ENJOYING THE JOURNEY

Enjoying the Journey

90 Spirit-Lifters for the Potholes of Life

Lois Olmstead

CHRISTIAN PUBLICATIONS, INC.
CAMP HILL, PENNSYLVANIA

Christian Publications, Inc.
3825 Hartzdale Drive
Camp Hill, PA 17011
www.cpi-horizon.com
www.christianpublications.com

Faithful, biblical publishing since 1883

Enjoying the Journey
ISBN: 0-87509-886-X

LOC Control Number: 00-135125

© 2001 by Christian Publications

Printed in the United States of America

01 02 03 04 05   5 4 3 2 1

Author photo by Rick Rivard's Photography

This book is dedicated to our three sons,

Todd,
Kevin
and Ross,

who are gifts to us from God.
You increased the joy on my life journey a hundredfold.
I love you guys. . . .
And I'm thankful that even when I write about you,
you still love me *too!*

Introduction

For Lois Olmstead, finding an adventure isn't too hard. She just looks from where she's standing.

"No matter where I live or what I'm doing, it is a new adventure," says Lois. "This is my Colstrip adventure." Lois, who along with her family has lived in Colstrip, Montana since 1973, began writing a column for *The Independent-Enterprise* and *The Rosebud County Press* called "Time Out With Lois."

The column covered a variety of subjects. It was her desire that the columns be inspirational, humorous and helpful to others seeking adventure in their lives. Inspiring others is something that has become part of her everyday life. For a number of years now Lois has been traveling all over the country sharing her faith in God and her views on life in general. She is highly sought as an inspirational speaker. "I love to travel and share that my faith in God is not just for Sundays, Christmas and Easter," she said. Her invitations usually come from someone who heard her speak somewhere before or heard about her talks.

Born on a ranch north of Livingston, Lois met her husband, Robert, while he was an engineering student at Montana State University. They have been married thirty-nine years. "To be married to someone who loves you, is your best friend and encourages you and supports you continually is a blessing from God," says Lois. "Somewhere along the way, probably because of all our Northern Cheyenne friends, I started calling Robert 'He-who-takes-long-steps.' (He is six foot nine!) That got shortened to 'He-who.' I'm afraid if he gave me an Indian name it would be 'She-who-fears-the-kitchen'!" Lois and Robert have three grown sons, two daughters-in-law and three grandchildren. Lois likes to say, "I've raised three sons, one husband—and also twenty-four ducks!" (She is a certified duck-lover.)

Her husband retired from the Montana Power Company after thirty-two years of service and now enjoys running his own parts-finding business and working part-time at a Carquest store. During their marriage they have lived in several Montana cities. Lois has found a number of interesting "adventures" along the way. One was a three-year radio talk show in Billings, Montana, in which she interviewed personalities and gave homemaking tips. "They did not think it would work—a women's talk show in the 1970s. But it became pretty popular. Even men listened. Some of them were my biggest fans. One man, Bill Cline, listened every day as he drove the county grader."

Another adventure was opening a gift shop and art gallery called "Apple Cider Alley" when the family moved to Colstrip. A regular customer at the local café, the Coal Bowl (Lois has her own coffee mug there), she is also very active in community affairs, volunteers at the elementary school and is a Reach to Recovery volunteer. She is active in her local church, Colstrip Christian and Missionary Alliance. Lois believes that if you put your trust in God, you will find "strength, joy and peace." She writes her columns reflecting these ideals.

As Pat Corley, her editor at *Rosebud County Press* and *The Independent-Enterprise*, wrote,

Her columns, although filled with entertaining personal experiences, also contain a basic Christian message—and provide an opportunity for reflection and self-assessment.

Lois has a way of writing that makes the reader feel like "part of the family." Over the years we have shared experiences with her children, her friends, her family—and have seen the world uniquely through her eyes. We've shed tears, we've laughed—and we've seen our own reflections sometimes.

I feel fortunate to have been able to share Lois' talents with the readers of our newspapers. . . . She draws from a wealth of experiences in her own life and in the lives of her friends and family to provide a genuinely uplifting message. I hope, after reading her work, that you will wholeheartedly agree!

Day 1

Thereto My Troth

On September 15, 1961, a young (skinny) couple stood before their pastor and promised to pledge their troth. I still don't know what troth is. We said, "Whither thou goest I will go" and promised to stick together for richer or poorer and in sickness and health. Four days later we went back to college.

We were living at Old Faithful in Yellowstone Park on our first anniversary with our first son, Todd, who was three months old. Our second anniversary was spent in the park again, this time at Canyon Village. It was work in the summer and live up to the "poor" in our vows during the school year. Robert got a job with Montana Power after graduation. We moved to Rainbow Dam at Great Falls. Our third anniversary we could afford to go out to dinner. Kevin was a month old on our fourth anniversary. The seventh anniversary found us house hunting in Billings where Robert was transferred. On the eighth we praised God for the birth of our third son, Ross.

For two years we were in the same place. He was working at the steam plant and I was traveling around Montana giving sewing lessons. We gave each other cards for our ninth anniversary since we had just bought a house. On our eleventh anniversary the house was for sale. We were moving to Colstrip.

On our eighteenth we didn't know whether to go out or not. The boys thought they were too old for a sitter and we didn't. On our twenty-fifth the boys hosted a surprise celebration. This year we celebrated our thirty-eighth anniversary with dinner at home—a real switch.

With the grace of God, He has blessed our vows. We have tested whither-thou-goest, richer and poorer, and in-sickness and in-health. If I was asked today, "Do you take this man . . . ?" I would say, "Positively, joyfully, I do!" (And he can still keep my troth too!)

Read
1 Timothy 3

My prayer of joy for today:

(This space is provided in each day's reading for you to jot down a short response to what God is saying to your heart today about joy.)

Brick by Brick

A group of people tried to build a tower that would reach into heaven: "And they said one to another, Go to, let us make brick, and burn them thoroughly. And they had brick for stone, and slime had they for mortar. And they said, Go to, let us build us a city and a tower, whose top may reach unto heaven" (Genesis 11:3-4, KJV).

Don't hasten to laugh. We do the same thing. I did the same thing. Oh, I didn't know I was making bricks. I was just trying to be good—good enough to please God. I was building my own little tower: A brick of teaching Sunday school followed by a brick of nursery duty. A brick of being Christian Women's Club (CWC) decorations chairman and even a brick of taking baked beans to the potluck church suppers now and then!

The things that were really important to me were looking good and being good. However, at age twenty-six, this nice church lady got to doing some serious thinking—and watching and listening. I started watching the speakers at CWC, the other gals on the committee and the women in my church. I started listening to Christian radio. I started listening, really listening, to the sermons at my church. I started thinking about Bible verses that I had memorized years before. I started studying my Bible—for me.

I memorized a verse years ago that said, "For no one can lay any foundation other than the one already laid, which is Jesus Christ" (1 Corinthians 3:11). I could stack all the bricks I wanted but those good-works bricks wouldn't do. I had memorized this one too: "For by grace are ye saved through faith; and that not of yourselves: it is the gift of God: not of works [i.e., VBS, CWC, church, etc.], lest any man should boast" (Ephesians 2:8-9, KJV). Right there I saw myself trying to be good enough for God. The Bible says, "All have sinned, and come short of the glory of God" (Romans 3:23, KJV). Even church ladies.

Then I made a realization. God had a blueprint for me. It was even on Christmas cards. "For unto you is born this day in the city of David a Saviour, which is Christ the Lord" (Luke 2:11, KJV).

I knelt beside my bed. I said through tears, "Forgive me for trying to do it my way. Jesus, come into my life. You be in charge. I will follow Your building plans from now on, believing that You are who You say You are and that Your Word, the Bible, is for me." Remembering my former cowgirl days I said, "I am turning the reins over to you."

My life is different because of that day. I am here to tell you—God never fails! He gives peace. He gives comfort and joy. In storms, He causes the clouds to part and the sun to shine through. He has a plan. I trust Him. He is putting the bricks together now and He is the Master Builder. That gives me joy!

Read
Genesis 11

My prayer of joy for today:

It's Just a Machine

At one of my jobs I spent many hours with the computer, which I named Nebuchadnezzar. For a while, I thought he had something against me. I figured Nebuchadnezzar was determined to make me look stupid—which he did. It didn't take long for me to discover one of my basic operating errors: thinking the computer is human.

"Why did you do that?" I asked the computer. "That's not what I meant."

He just sat there looking at me, blinking, "Invalid command." I was about to say it was *not* the wrong command when I realized I was talking to a machine. A *machine.*

I had to be more careful. People were starting to look at me strangely when I was talking to the inanimate object on my desk. I don't think you are supposed to have physical contact with the screen either. I caught myself stretching out my finger to show Nebuchadnezzar which figures I wanted in a certain place when he asked me: "Command?"

Hitting him is out too.

Nebuchadnezzar had a partner—the printer. The first time I endeavored to print out some reports, it launched an attack. I pressed "print." It started spitting out the reports. And spitting out reports. And more reports. And more reports. I did what any new, trying-to-make-a-good-impression, conscientious employee would do. I leaned against the wall in a fit of giggles.

I could just picture the entire office flooded with reports—over the desk, the files, washing out the door into the streets in front of the Colstrip Community Service's office. The picture was hilarious—to me.

My boss walked over to the printer and pressed "Cancel." The flood of reports stopped immediately. As I was trying to gain control I said, "Well, I could paper my family room with these if you want me to take them home. . . ."

I tried to place the blame on Nebuchadnezzar, but of course he left the evidence glowing on the screen in neon-green letters that I had not given him the right commands. Humph!

I have to remind myself that he is just a machine, but sometimes Nebuchadnezzar makes it difficult. He developed a problem yesterday that we couldn't figure out and we had to call the company computer department. When we asked what had gone wrong, the programmer said, "Oh sometimes the computer just gets confused."

Sure, it's just a machine. I still think I'll put Nebuchadnezzar on my "People to Pray For" list.

Read
Daniel 3

My prayer of joy for today:

Day 4

Leave It Alone, Lois

I had just finished speaking at a retreat session when a young lady came up to me and asked, "Do you have a favorite verse or saying?"

I stammered a bit and said, "Well, I do . . . but I better explain it. My saying is 'Leave it alone, Lois.' "

She said, "Yes, you better explain it."

Then I told her. I was eighteen feet up in the air on a scaffold helping to perfa-tape the dome ceiling in our church. Many volunteers were there during the day. We had just come up after a coffee break that had included an intense discussion on which rooms in the church should be locked and which ones left open. The day before we had had a carpet discussion. I had, of course, been vocal in my opinion both times.

Now, from my lofty perch, I could hear some ladies discussing whether we should have drapes or blinds on the windows. I put my goop-covered trowel down and started to climb off the scaffold. *I've got to get down there and tell them what I think,* I thought to myself.

Just then it felt like a hand grabbed my shoulder. I felt absolutely stopped in my tracks. (After all, I was kinda in the heavens up there!) It seemed a voice clear as a lightning bolt said, "Leave it alone, Lois."

I sat back down on my perch with my heart pounding. Wow! I thought about it. "Leave it alone, Lois"? That made a lot of sense. Why did I think I had to have a say about the drapes? For that matter, why did I think I had to have an opinion about everything? Just who did I think I was? Wow!

I went back to my task at hand—humbled and repentant. *Forgive me, Lord,* I prayed. *And thank You for loving me enough to help me with my shortcomings. I will always try to keep this message in mind.*

The lady to whom I was relating this was understanding and seemed so interested. She said she'd see me later and I went on to the next workshop. The next evening was the end of the retreat. God had met our hearts in a special way. We were preparing to go home uplifted and encouraged. A knock on my cabin door interrupted my packing. It was the same gal with a package in her hand. "I want you to open this when you get home." I thanked her and put it in my suitcase.

Can you imagine how I felt when I tore the paper off a beautiful work of art? On heavy pink paper she had carefully sketched mountains. They were the backdrop for perfectly shaped letters with the message, "Leave it alone, Lois." Naturally I wanted to preserve this beautiful gift. I took it to a professional framer. I was elated with the finished job. I wanted to be reminded of my "message" from God. It is so easy for me to forget things! If you see me walking around with a framed pink picture under my arm, don't laugh. I am just taking lessons!

Read
1 Chronicles 16:7-12

My prayer of joy for today:

Day 5

Hinge Pins of Joy

"Dad, what do you think a hinge pin is?" We were sitting in the living room at the ranch where I grew up. I was in a rocker made from four-foot pine logs sitting right in front of the wood stove. It is my favorite place.

"You mean like a piano hinge?"

"I don't know; that's why I am asking you. I have an idea what a hinge pin is, but I'm not sure I'm right."

"Well, it's that pin that runs down through the hinge to keep it in place. The hinge turns on it."

"Great! That is exactly what I thought!" He looked at me like I was getting awfully excited about an incidental little thing. "I need it for the book," I explained.

And it is *not* an incidental little thing. The hinge pin. The hinge would not work without it. It allows the gate to do what it is supposed to do—swing. Get a mental picture.

- The gate post = strong, buried deep, solid, stable, reliable, trustworthy, firm

- The gate = dependent upon the post, has a purpose

- The hinges = fasten the gate post and the gate together

- The hinge pins = small, yet the key, the means by which the gate swings

Do you get the picture? God, us, the cross and His precepts. *The doctrines and principles upon which we walk in faith are my hinge pins.*

> Then we will no longer be infants, tossed back and forth by the waves, and blown here and there by every wind of teaching and by the cunning and craftiness of men in their deceitful scheming. Instead, speaking the truth in love, we will in all things grow up into him who is the Head, that is, Christ. From him the whole body, joined and held together by every supporting ligament, grows and builds itself up in love, as each part does its work. . . .
>
> You were taught, with regard to your former way of life, to put off your old self, which is being corrupted by its deceitful desires; *to be made new in the attitude of your minds; and to put on the new self, created to be like God in true righteousness and holiness.* (Ephesians 4:14-16, 22-24, emphasis added)

Do you get the picture? God, the cross, His precepts and us. God, the Father; God, the Son, Jesus Christ; God, the Holy Spirit; and us. *Rejoice!*

Read
Hebrews 10:10-22

My prayer of joy for today:

Day 6

Where There Is Smoke

For several years I worked for Colstrip Community Services as a receptionist and accounting clerk. It was like the city hall of our town and a great place to work. We handled the water, streets and sewer services plus the rental of company-owned apartments and mobile home lots. It was a great learning experience for me.

It was also a great learning experience for them. They learned the columns I wrote about my cooking disasters were true. I was just making an afternoon popcorn snack using the microwave in the administration building kitchen. I put it in and ran back to answer the phone in our office. I heard the smoke alarm before I saw the smoke. I went running to the kitchen. (I am used to doing that from my kitchen alarm experience at home.) The microwave was billowing clouds of smoke. Evidently the numbers on the dial read differently than ours at home. There was black smoke coming out of the microwave and an awful stench. But the worst thing happened next.

Red and blue lights started flashing. Mike Ames, head of security, came through the door. When he saw the source of the problem, he called off the fire engines. We opened the doors and got the bag of burned hulls out of the microwave and into the trash outside. The entire building stank. And everyone on site at the generating plants knew there had been an emergency call. God did hear my frantic prayer, "Please don't let the automatic sprinklers come on and douse everyone!" I would have never lived that down.

The safety report that came to our office the next morning simply stated, "Fire, smoke, Lois, kitchen." Oh, how tough it is to live with a reputation! It is a wonder I have any joy left. Thank You, Jesus!

**Read
Luke 24**

My prayer of joy for today:

A Bus Ride

Since the roads were icy, I decided to ride the bus home from the ranch. I boarded with my coffee mug, the newspaper and some emergency gummy bears. A young mother and her little girl, about four years old, were in the seat across the aisle. The little girl slept on her mother's lap for about an hour, then woke up and started pestering her mom.

"When are we going to get there? When can I see Daddy? I'm tired of riding this bus. Where is my daddy?"

The mom got out some dry cereal for a treat. "Daddy is in Billings, temporarily. We will see him there." The questions were repeated many times. I gave the little girl the comics from my newspaper to look at. That interested her for a while. Then the questions poured out again. I felt sorry for the mom.

"Where are you from?" I asked.

"Butte," she said.

"Wow, you have been on this bus a long time," I said.

"We're going to Billings to see my daddy," said the little girl as she jumped off her seat and came over to stand by me. She turned to her mom, "Is he still in jail?"

"Yes," the mom answered.

"How long can we see Daddy?"

"Just till the bus goes back tonight. I have to be at work to-morrow. We'll have a couple hours. We'll get a taxi when we get there. Come back to your seat."

I asked the mom if the little girl could have some sweets and shared my gummy bears when she said it was OK. I started praying immediately for this family. *Lord, show me what to do, what to say.* Riding a bus from Butte to Billings had to take at least six hours. With a four-year-old, for a two-hour visit and then back on the bus to ride back to Butte? In the same day? I kept praying. The mother and daughter were leaning on each other with their eyes closed.

The bus depot in Billings was packed with people. I watched the young mom and her daughter go to the phone. Then they stood on the sidewalk. Later I saw the mom come in and call on the phone again. Then back outside. It had been nearly forty minutes. Still no taxi.

Now, if you're the type of person who can sit placidly through this scene, I applaud you. Me? I was going nuts. What could she do? What could *I* do? I didn't have a car; I couldn't help. I prayed again. *Lord, PLEASE!* Just then they called my bus for boarding. I glanced back. Praise the Lord. They were getting into a taxi.

When I got settled into my seat, I found myself crying. My heart was breaking for that little family. I prayed some more. *Lord, I just didn't know what to do for them.* The situation seemed totally closed. There was no opening to share. I felt like a failure.

In a few moments, I felt a sense of peace. Who was I to feel praying was not enough in this situation? God does hear our prayers. I believe it. On that day, I had to rest in that.

Read
Hebrews 11:1-6

My prayer of joy for today:

Day 8

How Do We Do It?

Holding the little green book in my hands was like step-ping back in time. Twenty-six years ago this was my journal. Some days I had only time to make a list. Other days I poured my heart out on paper sprinkled with tears. Our family had just moved to Colstrip that year. The boys were twelve, nine and six. Little did I know what would fill those pages. We lived in one of two newly constructed apartment build-ings. There was no paved street—only a clay road. Robert put up a sign outside our dwelling: "Keep Off the Grass." It an-nounced his type of humor. (There was no grass.)

We felt like pioneers. That must have been the reason for my choice of a verse for the year. I wrote it on the first page of the little green book: "Thou wilt keep him in perfect peace, whose mind is stayed on thee" (Isaiah 26:3, KJV).

As I scanned the pages of the journal, I realized how God kept this promise. An entry for August 7, 1974 follows:

> Today I cleaned house, washed and dried six loads of clothes, had devotions with Todd, washed camping dishes, made a relish tray for a Bible study luncheon where I gave devotions. Made seven calls to set up programs for radio interviews in Billings on Friday. In the afternoon, I went to a Tupperware party, visited a new neighbor, took boys swimming in the old swimming hole and swam too. I put in roast beef and fixed potatoes and gravy for dinner. Before

Robert came home, I washed the car and then took a shower. Such is the life in a normal day for a Colstrip homemaker-pioneer.

Whew! Sitting here twenty-six years later, I get tired just reading that. Was I really that busy? Did I really have that much energy? I know that did not happen every day because I read the rest of the little green book. There were days when nothing major got accomplished. Yet somehow, in the midst of it all, we made it! The clothes did get washed, the children did get fed and we all survived! Amazing—no, miraculous!

The real truth, the reason that the homemaker-pioneer can sit in the quiet, calm, peaceful atmosphere of our home today and look back fondly to those days is because she knows the Source of the strength and the secret of survival of those days. She knows the freedom of forgiveness for the not-so-great times.

If you feel like a pioneer in your life, if your days are so full you feel you are on an express train, if you don't know how you can make it through another day, stop—and listen to me. . . .

I believe I know how you feel. Take my hand. I want you to know you can make it if you trust God. Trust God. Trust Him simply to do what He says He will do in His Word. He will care for you. He does know and He understands what you are going through.

Please allow me to give you a gift today. Could I give you my verse for you to hang on to? Here it is.

Read
Isaiah 26:3

My prayer of joy for today:

Day 9

Aunt Ruth

My great-aunt Ruth Bohleen was one of the first Christian and Missionary Alliance missionaries to the Philippines. She said, "We weren't rich in material things, but we were rich in love and blessings from God. Mother and Dad took us to church and Sunday school . . . and stayed."

Her long boat trip to the mission field began on December 17, 1927. Her experiences there became an inspiration to me as I grew up. A boy came to her door at six on a Monday morning with the news of the bombing of Pearl Harbor. The small group of missionaries met in a home to pray and plan. The story of the trip into the interior of the island to hide is heart-wrenching. Yet the year spent at a rustic mountain camp was filled with inspiring and courageous adventures. She said, "A baby was born during that time named Victor Glen Hess. We had named our refuge 'Victory Glen.' "

When they were discovered, the camp was burned and they were herded down the mountain. They were being loaded into the hold of a rat-infested boat for the trip to a prison camp. She told me, "I can still see one of our small Filipino boys standing on the shore. He cupped his hands to his mouth and shouted, 'Romans 8:28!' to us as we went out to sea. Truly God was with us."

The small group of missionaries were housed in a dance hall with hundreds of political prisoners. Yet she wrote, "I will never forget that time. There were the most beautiful sunsets I ever saw in my life there. God was good to us during those hard times." Often near starvation, her faith was strong. She met Rob Dickson, a school teacher. He had narrowly escaped being murdered. The grave for him had already been dug when his life was spared. The story of their rescue, marriage and life together serving the Lord was told and retold in my family. Learning their secret—finding joy and blessing in the midst of the bad times (even prison camp!)—is one of the foundational bricks of faith and joy in my life.

Read
1 Corinthians 2

My prayer of joy for today:

Skinny and Perfectly Organized (Part I)

The clerk started sliding the items from my cart across the grocery store scanner. There was oven cleaner, floor wax and dusting spray. There were products that clean the tile in the bathroom and stuff for the windows and mirrors. Appliance cleaner slid across behind the sink cleanser. Then sponges and brushes to help me apply all this stuff.

"You must be into spring cleaning," mentioned the clerk.

"No," I said, "I just got back from visiting my friend Karen. She is such a neat housekeeper!"

Just then she picked up another one of my purchases, a six-pack of a chocolate diet drink. "Does this work?" she asked.

"I don't know," I said, "but Karen is skinny too."

I had just returned from a trip to Texas, which was a birthday gift from my husband. Karen and I had a wonderful reunion. Texas was beautiful. The bluebonnets were in bloom. The week flew by as we took trips to Fredericksburg and Austin. We shopped. Karen had a luncheon so I could meet many of her friends. With laughter and tears we encouraged each other, sharing our victories and happenings from over the last four years since we had seen each other.

Yet I discovered something about myself. I can still be a victim of peer pressure. At my age, I still have not attained total self-acceptance. I wish I were skinnier, like Karen. I wish I were as organized as she is. We were waiting for my plane in Dallas when Karen asked, "Lois, do you have a book to read on the plane?"

"Are you kidding? I won't read a book. I have my notebook. I have to make lists—of cleaning supplies to buy, goals for diet and exercise . . . I have to set up a weekly household schedule. I need to make a budget. I need to make a list! I want to be like you!"

We both laughed. I am glad I got this vacation. I came home renewed, rested, refreshed and, yes, inspired to continue working on me. (Husbands, take note!)

As I left the grocery store with my cleaning supplies and diet food, I breathed a prayer to God. "Lord, thank You for the new challenges I feel in my role as a woman. But let me never forget that what is inside counts most. And even if I still don't get skinny or perfectly organized, I know You love me. Make me content with who I am. I can live with that. Thank You, God."

Read
1 Thessalonians 2

My prayer of joy for today:

Attack Worry with a Pencil

Right now, right where you are sitting, stop and ask yourself, "Do I have worries that are destroying my joy?" Do you have wrinkles across your forehead as you go through your day? Is your stomach in knots? Is there a nagging headache that won't go away? Do you wish you could just take some people, sit them down and tell them how things really ought to be done? Worry does not build joy and peace. The very need to control comes from our old flesh, the self we gave to God when we came to Him. It comes naturally to the natural man. We who belong to the family of God are no longer natural—we are spiritual. The spirit of God dwells within us.

Worry comes as a temptation from our enemy to defeat our trust in God. This temptation can be a battle. With any battle, we need to grab our weapons and gather the soldiers. We need to fight. Read Ephesians 6:10-18 for getting equipped.

It might be a helpful exercise for us to write down a list of our worries. Put the evasive little bullets of the enemy down on paper. Then study the list. Circle the things that you have no control over. This will take some evaluating and thoughtful consideration. Then offer these circled concerns to the Lord in prayer. Write across those concerns *Given to God* and the date. Then go back over your list. There are the other worries. Pray for wisdom. What can you do to change the situation? Do you need to list a series of steps you need to take to get out of this problem? Do it. Do you need to go talk to someone to mend a broken friendship? Do it.

If your worry is the budget, or the lack of one, tackle it today. Seek help if you need it. If it is a health issue you are trying to avoid, make an appointment. Do it. Realize that the color of worry is gray, never really black or white. When we move it from gray to black and white, it is no longer worry. It is an enemy we have defeated and taken captive. Now let the restoration begin. Have a parade. Sing a song of victory. Wave the flag of joy. Faith comes by hearing and hearing by the Word of God (see Romans 10:17, KJV)! Praise our King!

Read
Luke 12:16-34

My prayer of joy for today:

Skinny and Perfectly Organized (Part II)

I want to report that I have used all those cleaning supplies I bought. I told you how a trip to visit my friend Karen spurred me into action. She has a job outside the home and her house was still so clean. I made a list while on the plane trip home of all the household chores I had been neglecting. I went to the store and bought everything I had seen advertised on TV that is guaranteed to make your home sparkle.

I sure have been busy. I cleaned the closets and cupboards. I went through my pantry. I scrubbed walls and floors. I washed windows and curtains. I moved furniture and dusted the bookshelves. I even gathered my courage and threw stuff out. The china teapot that goes with our good china dishes had a broken spout. We were given these dishes as wedding gifts well over thirty years ago. I don't know why I was keeping it. I had another teapot, given to me by a friend. Her little boy knocked it off the shelf of a fancy gift shop and the store made her pay for it. "I know it has a crack in it and no lid," she said, "but I thought you could use it for flower arrangements.

It would go with your decor." The little boy is a seventh grader this year. I threw it out too.

I organized my kitchen cupboards. I even washed all the shelves and oiled the doors before I put the stuff back in. I cleaned the stove and oven. I saw a sale in the Billings paper on wallpaper. I drove the 260-mile round-trip and the next day redecorated the kitchen walls. It looks so good I might even learn to cook now.

I also told you my friend was skinny. I had bought several cans of diet drink at the same time I bought my cleaning supplies. However, they are still here. I got so hungry doing all this cleaning that I really felt I needed to eat to keep my strength up. So I am not skinny yet. As a matter of fact I went to get a hot fudge sundae yesterday (a reward for working so hard cleaning the utility room). I got the mail while I was downtown.

There was a letter from my friend in Texas. She gets the paper and had read my column. She thanked me for all the nice things I had said about her. She told me how much she enjoyed my visit. She was flattered that I thought she was skinny. And then she wrote, "Lois, I feel that I have to tell you . . . I have a cleaning lady." I was so relieved.

You know, this cleaning business could have turned into a habit. I feel so good today. I am sitting in a spotlessly clean house contemplating drinking that diet stuff tomorrow.

Read
Proverbs 31

My prayer of joy for today:

Day 13

Breast Cancer Awareness

In 1992, when I was diagnosed with a malignant tumor, the statistics were one in nine women in the United States would get breast cancer in their lifetime. Now, one in eight women will be stricken with the disease. Men are also susceptible to this cancer.

Today there is not only better screening for tumors, but people are also becoming more conscious of the advantages of regular prescreening tests for many types of cancer. Early detection is the best defense.

That year when I made the trek to the clinic for my annual physical, my doctor checked me over and then we were to return in the afternoon for results of all the tests. "You can go down and get your mammogram and chest x-ray. I will see you at 3 this afternoon," he said. "Everything looks fine so far."

When Robert and I went back in at 3 p.m., we learned everything was not fine. The films from my mammogram were up on the wall in my doctor's office. He told us that he had checked over my previous year's film. There was no trace of the tumor that showed up vividly this year. Surgery, chemotherapy and radiation resulted from my cancer diagnosis.

People blessed me and my family with prayers and support during that time. God became our Rock on which we stood during the storm. We thank Him daily for His grace to us and ask special blessings for the families of those who have not survived the cancer battle. In the Bible, Jesus did not raise every person who died, nor did He always divide the Red Sea, but today God gives us strength to walk through the storm, whether He parts the clouds or not.

There are many ways to fight in the battle against breast cancer. Pray. Volunteer at your local cancer center. Give. Wear your pink ribbon and reach out to offer support to someone around you with cancer who needs a gift of joy at this time. Pray that God will lead you where He wants you to go.

Read
Psalm 118

My prayer of joy for today:

Day 14

Stand Ye Still

JOY HINGE PIN

"Behold, God is my salvation; I will trust, and not be afraid: for the LORD JEHOVAH is my strength and my song; he also is become my salvation. Therefore with joy shall ye draw water out of the wells of salvation." (Isaiah 12:2-3, KJV)

"Ye shall not need to fight in this battle: set yourselves, stand ye still, and see the salvation of the LORD with you, O Judah and Jerusalem: fear not, nor be dismayed; to morrow go out against them: for the LORD will be with you." (2 Chronicles 20:17, KJV)

This last verse became real to me during my battle with breast cancer. Again and again when I wanted to activate, push, stew or pressure the doctors, my family or God, I was reminded of this verse. Hundreds of times when circumstances were not what I wanted them to be, I heard the quiet voice of the Holy Spirit repeating this verse to me.

I am a do-er and a fixer. This was probably one of the hardest lessons of my cancer walk—*Set yourself. Stand still. See the salvation of the Lord with you!*

God constantly brought this verse to mind. I believe it will be with me through my life. It is a joy hinge pin. Without it, we swing from side to side, tossed to and fro by every circumstance.

By God's grace and mercy and with His strength, fear was not a constant companion during cancer treatment. There were attacks of fear that I recognized immediately. I dealt with them as if in warfare. Others were subtle. But an overall fear for my life was dealt with through God's promises and His direction, "Stand still." I wrote the book *Breast Cancer and Me* as evidence. In living with cancer and in dying with cancer, God is there—if you invite Him, as your Lord and Savior, to be there. God is able.

This is true for our life walk. Standing still is the opposite of running wildly through life trying to find joy in material possessions, fame and acclaim and riches. Standing still is an act of submission. Standing still with eyes focused on our Lord God Almighty puts us on the high road, the narrow road, the road leading to eternity with Him. *We are to stand still and listen for His voice.* That is a joy hinge pin.

Read
1 Samuel 9:27; Job 37:14; Psalms 4:4; 46:10

My prayer of joy for today:

Day 15

Bye-Bye, Dream

Sometimes one must give certain dreams up and kiss a lifetime goal good-bye. I am working through that process right now. It is not easy. It has long been one of my dreams to work in the safety/training field. It would work so well with my business of giving motivational workshops for health care facilities, community service groups, etc. The Montana Power Company and Western Energy Company near where I live have been my primary corporate targets. *Someday I will get a call. I just know it,* I often told myself.

But one has to be realistic. This is just not going to happen. I blew my chances with Western Energy. Most everyone that works for the mining company already knows this (at least any of those at the mine who had their two-way radios on that day). You see, I was backup tour guide for the Colstrip Visitor Center. That day we had sixty small-business owners from all over the United States. They came in two huge touring buses to Colstrip for the mine tour. Vicki was the tour guide in one bus. I had the other. I am not going over the humiliating details, but I lost the other bus in the mine.

The workers at the mine were so helpful. They were calling each other across the mine on their two-way radios, "Have you seen the other bus? Lois has lost the other bus!"

Of course they'd call back, "Yes, we see a bus. Is it the blue and green one?"

"No, that is the one Lois is in." (And I was all over that mine looking for the other bus, so naturally every worker in the several-thousand acre mine had seen me and my bus!) "We are looking for the purple one."

Eventually we found each other. These poor people had been on the one-hour tour for two hours! Needless to say, I had covered my standard tour facts in the first hour. The rest of the stuff I made up! The only consolation of that ordeal was that I got two job offers off the bus! They said if I could keep thirty-six businesspeople entertained for two hours and not have them crying to get off the bus, they could find a place for me *somewhere* in their companies.

I rather doubt Western Energy will be calling me anytime soon to go to work in their safety/training department. Oh well, my joy does not depend on my dreams all coming true. My joy depends on God's still loving me—even when I blow it!

Read Luke 15

My prayer of joy for today:

Dressing Inside Out

A s I got dressed for work one day, a sermon just popped into my mind. It concerned my clothes. As I checked in the mirror, my red dress was perfect. The buttons were all sewed on and the gold earrings and bracelet I had chosen were exquisite. My slip wasn't showing. That was a good thing because I had had to staple a couple inches of lace in the back hem where I had caught my heel in it. My undergarments were in pretty good shape but a little tattered here and there. I had a run in my nylons. But I caught it before it went below the knee. A dab of pink nail polish (I didn't have clear) stopped it from running any further.

This little sermon floated right out of my mirror, scooting into my soul. "How often, Lois, do you look perfect on the outside, but underneath you are tattered and desperately in need of mending?" Sometimes when we look the best we are desperately in need of help. We dress up to cover our hurts and insecurities.

Wouldn't it be interesting if we all came to church wearing on the outside what we felt on the inside? We would have some tattered shirts, some runs in our socks, some safety pins barely holding us together. There would be seams ready to burst with frustration, despair and worry. Of course there would be flowery prints and bright colors too. There would be silks and satins, purple velvets and soft white wool.

How about you? How would you dress inside out today? We worship One who knows our hearts. We can turn to Him knowing He already knows us inside out. That gives me joy.

Read
1 John 3

My prayer of joy for today:

My Agenda

"I've got a plan," I said to Robert. "If *we* would each spend an hour at *our* desks tonight after supper, *we* could get through those piles of mail and stuff."

He responded, "That would be a good idea." That took courage on his part. Going through piles of mail and stuff is his least favorite thing to do.

After supper, I washed the dishes. We do not have a dishwasher in our country home. (I wanted to see if I could change into a nicer woman because I spend time with my hands in dishwater.) He-who-takes-long-steps was sitting in his chair in the living room. "Well, let's hit the desks," I said very cheerfully after finishing the dishes. I headed down the hall to my hovel.

The first thing I had to do was get birthday presents ready to mail. The hands-in-dishwater stint must not work right away, because I was thinking, *Why do mothers always have to remember the dates, figure out a plan, buy the presents, wrap the presents and mail the presents?*

Then I went through the health insurance stuff, which was very confusing but I got it done. It did run through my mind that this task had always been mine. Years ago, standing at the altar, I must have said "I do" to some small-print items I didn't hear. After I got through my pile of magazine renewals and recent photos that needed to go into albums (has He-who ever put pictures in albums?), I decided I better get a cool glass of water . . . and an attitude adjustment.

He was in the library in the desk chair when I walked by. He was playing computer games. At my glance (well, my murderous look), he said, "I'm just getting warmed up for the desk." I humpffed my way back to my hovel and expertly, with a sense of purpose, worked at my desk until it was clean down to the desk pad. I filed all the mail. I cleaned off my computer desk. Then I sorted through some cards. I was finding I had energy to burn ("burn" being the key word). I took two more trips to the kitchen. I didn't even look. (Well, I did look, and He-who was still at the computer.)

"Here is the letter I typed," he said later. I was surprised he dared venture into my "warm" hovel. "Do you want to file a copy?"

The next day when I came home from work, I noticed the rolltop was up on his desk in the library. It looked like it had been spit-polished. The in-basket on top of his desk was empty. I don't know why I got in such a flap about it all. He told me he was "going to get around to it." He just wasn't doing it on my timetable. Hmmmm. Methinks I better spend some more time with my hands in the dishwater—and my mind on being joyful—in all things, especially at home!

Read
Psalm 92

My prayer of joy for today:

38

Day 18

Dishrags and Other Stuff

My friend Marita had her fingers bandaged the other day when I saw her. "I burned my fingers when I was taking a hot pan off the stove," she explained. "My oven mitt had a hole in it. I always fold it over but I forgot." I could relate to that. My potholders have holes in them too. "The ones I use every day are quite spiritual—holey!" We laughed. "I have new ones that were given to me as gifts . . . but they are too pretty to use. They hang over my stove!"

Isn't that stupid? Yet we all do it. We save the "good" stuff, the "new" stuff. One friend told me that she learned her lesson on that issue a long time ago. Her mother always saved the new dishes, the new towels and the new sheets. She used the "old" stuff. Then she died. After a time her husband remarried and the "new" wife used all the "new" stuff.

"That was it for me," my friend said. "Now I use it all."

This is probably good advice for all of us. Take this simple test. How do you rate?

1. 5 points for every potholder that is worn thin or holey.

2. 10 points for every new sheet or towel set you are saving.

3. 10 points for every appliance cord that you have to wiggle just right to get the appliance to run.

4. 5 points for every appliance that has a broken leg or knob. (My friend, Sharon, propped her electric frypan on a mea-

suring cup for four years because the leg was broken. "Otherwise, it was perfectly good," she said.)

5. 20 points if you have to slap your toast down four times before the toaster works.

6. 10 points for every key that you are keeping that you have no idea what it fits.

7. 10 points for every load of clothes you normally dry without checking the lint filter.

8. 10 points for every string of Christmas lights you have for which a) bulbs are no longer available, or b) they just don't work and you don't know why.

9. One point for each hole in your everyday dishrags and add them to your total.

10. 10 points for each sock by the washing machine that does not have a mate.

Key: 30-50 points: You are doing a good job. Make yourself a cup of tea.

60-90 points: You have some work to do. Go room by room, including the garage, taking care of the hazards. Put out some new potholders. Now have a cup of tea.

100 points and over: You are in serious trouble. Read Matthew 6:19-34. Get your priorities in order. Then report to the nearest safety seminar you can find. Check yourself in.

Read
Proverbs 4

My prayer of joy for today:

Day 19

Call unto Me—in Joy

ȜOY HINGE PIN

*"Hitherto have ye asked nothing in my name:
ask, and ye shall receive, that your joy may be full."
(John 16:24, KJV)*

It has taken many years for me to realize the privilege of praying with God. I have never talked with a president of the United States. I have never spoken with an earthly king. I doubt I could get permission if I wanted to. Yet, God, my Lord, my Redeemer, King of kings and Coming King, not only permits me to talk with Him, but also gives me an open invitation.

- "Seek the LORD and his strength, seek his face continually." (1 Chronicles 16:11, KJV)

- "And it shall come to pass, that before they call, I will answer; and while they are yet speaking, I will hear." (Isaiah 65:24, KJV)

- "Call unto me, and I will answer thee, and show thee great and mighty things, which thou knowest not." (Jeremiah 33:3, KJV)

- "Pray without ceasing. In every thing give thanks: for this is the will of God in Christ Jesus concerning you." (1Thessalonians 5:17-18, KJV)

Not only does God invite us to praise and pray with Him, but He also helps us when we don't know what to do, what to say or where to turn.

- "Likewise the Spirit also helpeth our infirmities: for we know not what we should pray for as we ought: but the Spirit itself maketh intercession for us with groanings which cannot be uttered. And he that searcheth the hearts knoweth what is the mind of the Spirit, because he maketh intercession for the saints according to the will of God." (Romans 8:26-27, KJV)

Our prayers are precious to God. "And when he had taken the book, the four beasts and four and twenty elders fell down before the Lamb, having every one of them harps, and golden vials full of odours, which are the prayers of saints" (Revelation 5:8, KJV).

Can you believe it? Amazing! Miraculous! I fall on my knees before my God. He hears me! I whisper a prayer. He hears me! I cry a request. He answers me! I sing praises to Him. *He hears me!* That is foundational to my overwhelming joy!

Read
2 Chronicles 7:14; Jeremiah 29:12; Isaiah 43

My prayer of joy for today:

42

A Day of Rest (Part 1)

Everett Hunter's Union 76 gas station was where we filled up when I was a teenager. We had to put gas in my parents' car in order to cruise the drag, which—of course—was our main reason for living. The drag in Livingston was one city block. We circled it for hours, never thinking it strange that this activity was the center of our relationships. Occasionally, we would cruise to the A&W, where carhops would envy our freedom as they took our orders for frosted glasses of 15-cent root beer. Then back to the drag to see if anyone new (of the opposite sex) was in our circling.

We would circle some more. This would necessitate a trip to refuel. We'd pool our funds, come up with a dollar and get four gallons of gas. Then we'd be back to the drag again until our curfew waved the checkered flag.

On Sundays, the local gas station owners in town would rotate who was going to stay open. One gas station would be open on Sunday. Grocery store owners would take turns too. They did this as a service to travelers. Regular people knew to stock up on groceries and get their gas during the week. Stores were not open on Sunday, because Sunday was a day of rest.

Only those required to keep services open worked. Nurses, railroad people and dairy farmers did work on Sundays, as did policemen, bus drivers and a few other people. They were a minority group. They had taken Exodus 34:21 seriously: "Six days you shall labor, but on the seventh day you shall rest; even during the plowing season and harvest you must rest."

Read
Exodus 34

My prayer of joy for today:

Day 21

A Day of Rest (Part 2)

God rested. God, Creator, King of kings, Lord of lords, rested. Genesis 2:2 says, "By the seventh day God had finished the work he had been doing; so on the seventh day *he rested* from all his work" (emphasis added). We remember that. Some even know the next verse: "And God blessed the seventh day and made it holy, because on it *he rested* from all the work of creating that he had done" (2:3, emphasis added).

At first, we Christians kept our seventh day holy. We still planned ahead. Yet needing that pair of socks or a battery tore at our principles. OK, we shopped on Sunday when it was an emergency. Emergency was determined by desire and soon every desire was a need—an emergency. The business owners must have thought so too. "Open Sundays" signs became as numerous as the cars filling up at gas stations on that day.

Somehow, rest on Sunday became recreation. We rested on Sundays, after church, by recreating. That muddied the waters. If I love to garden, that is my rest and recreation, right? Then, if I love to plow, plowing is my recreation, right?

I am not that old. But in the last forty years we have done a complete turnaround. Oh, how we rest now! We go to the mall and make a marathon of Sunday shopping. Or we load up the four-wheelers, the camper, the boats, the picnic coolers and fill the truck with gas and head 120 miles to rest. We rest at a high speed, action-packed pace. Then we race home to unload everything, wash clothes, do homework and prepare for our new week. *Rested?*

Maybe mentally. But in our body? You be the judge of that. It is an interesting trip in my mind to think about what God meant when He said, "On the seventh day, *thou shalt rest."*

Hmmmmm. Must have been just for the olden days. . . .

Read
Leviticus 23

My prayer of joy for today:

Day 22

For the Faith of a Child

It was one of those special Sunday afternoons. Robert and I took our little grandson, Justin, to the park near our house. A little girl playing there liked our company as well. We visited with her as she played in the sand. Justin was delighted when he found out his new playmate was fearful of ants. So to prove the prowess of the male gender, he squished several ants in his hand.

But we live in a new era. Young women, even at the ripe age of five, are quick to prove their equality. Soon she was standing in front of us sticking two fingers into our faces.

"See," she showed us proudly, "I killed an ant!"

Then her face fell. She got a look of horror on her face. "Oh no! *God* made it!" I thought she was going to cry. But in a flash her bright little smile returned. She shrugged her tiny little shoulders, spreading her arms open wide. "I guess He'll just have to make some more!" And off she skipped.

Oh, for the faith of a child!

As Robert and I sat on the park bench watching the children play, we could sense God smiling. We remembered what Jesus told His disciples:

> At the same time came the disciples unto Jesus, saying, Who is the greatest in the kingdom of heaven? And Jesus called a little child unto him, and set him in the midst of

them, And said, Verily I say unto you, Except ye be converted and become as little children, ye shall not enter into the kingdom of heaven. Whosoever therefore shall humble himself as this little child, the same is greatest in the kingdom of heaven. And whoso shall receive one such little child in my name receiveth me. (Matthew 18:1-5, KJV)

Read
Luke 18:16-17

My prayer of joy for today:

Day 23

The County Fair

A h-h-h-h . . . the sights and sounds of a county fair! The baaing of sheep and oinking of hogs mix with the screams of the thrill-seekers on the newest stomach-twisting carnival ride. The whoops and hollers of the rodeo fans over at the arena echo past the newest farm machinery parked like a row of prehistoric monsters in a bright array of new paint.

The fresh smells of hay, cotton candy and popcorn mingle with the unpleasant aromas not so common to townsfolk. Country kids race on the midway, exhilarated by a rare taste of unsupervised freedom. Clean, well-shaped straw hats, bright western shirts and jeans are the costume of choice.

Camaraderie mixed with competition is a prize-winning recipe. And there are shelves filled with them—those special recipes, some handed down from those original fair-going pioneers. Shiny jars of marmalade and jam. Chocolate cakes melting from the heat but still tempting passersby. One booth has pumpkins and zucchini bigger than some of the hogs.

An exhibition hall is an exhibition hall is an exhibition hall. Some are log or wood-frame construction. Some are new metal buildings. Some are simply a cavernous tent. But they all are cooked up with the same ingredients: garden booths, clothing and art displays, hawkers selling the latest in cookware and eyeglass cleaners, and the must-see grade school exhibits. Cooked up is a good choice of words. Always hot, encouraging one to race to the 4-H kitchen to buy a cold drink, exhibition halls are the center of the county fair. You sign up for free stuff every year at every booth, usually winning only a call a month later to see if you want to buy siding for your house.

You've seen one, you've seen 'em all! Yet each county fair has an individuality created by a previous generation where gathering together was one of the most joyous times of the year. Though we move in a world totally different from the pioneers, the joy and excitement of the county fair has survived the onslaught of the high pressure life of today.

I have a feeling that Passover Week in the times when Jesus walked here on earth were very similar to our county fairs. Can't you just picture them? Listen. Smell. Wait. Yes, I hear the laughter of children. I heard the *baa* of a sheep. I smell something cooking. Do you want to walk with me? Maybe we'll be able to hear Jesus speak.

Read
Deuteronomy 16

My prayer of joy for today:

Diet Success

Oh, sweet victory. I had been doing so well on my healthy eating program that I had finally lost ten pounds. I was feeling on top of the world. I stopped at the library to pick up the latest weight-loss book. *This will be a good incentive for the next ten pounds!* I thought. Then I went to Jimmy's Café for lunch, taking the new book to read during lunch. I needed to reward myself. Naturally food was the first reward that came to mind.

I hadn't had the cheese and fat-laden super nacho plate since January. "That is what I will have," I told the waitress. "And I will have one of those chocolate cookies for dessert." No one else was in the restaurant during my lunch. It would be my own private celebration of diet victory. Oh-h-h, how good it was. I was in heaven. I propped my feet up on the chair across the table and settled in, reading my diet book and eating to my heart's content.

Just then the door opened and in walked my friend, Hugh Broadus. The Rosebud Creek rancher was my friend and former diet competitor. He had beat me five years in a row in a battle of who could lose the most weight between January 1 and Valentine's Day. Hugh had sabotaged every diet contest by sending me candy and leaving gift certificates for pie in every café in Colstrip. I had been wanting to see him. I wanted to hear, "Wow, you have really lost weight this year, Lois," from his lips. I had wanted him to know how disciplined I had been this year.

And there I was with a mountain of colorful calories dripping off my chin, reading a diet book with a huge chocolate cookie by my plate! Drats! He didn't have to say a word. I could feel my face flaming in embarrassment. He joined me at the table. I could hardly talk. An old saying, "Your sins will find you out!" wafted through my brain.

"Did God send you?" I asked, quickly pushing the diet book under my purse. The next forkful of my victory lunch tasted flat and oh so heavy. His eyes had already seen the cookie. No sense in trying to hide it.

"Why?" he asked. I explained my victory lunch. He ordered a cheeseburger—only to make me feel better. The waitress refilled our coffee and brought over the bag of cookies I had ordered to take home with me for Robert. The sack seemed to glow as it sat on the table between us. Finally it was time to go.

I will just tell you this: The next time I hold a victory celebration, it is going to be in my closet at home! There is a moral to this story. You should have caught it by now.

Read
Proverbs 10

My prayer of joy for today:

The Long Way Around

Soon it will be vacation time. My friend, Phyllis, had company last week: her sister, Linda, and her husband, Rick, who live in Ohio. I went over to visit the morning they were leaving. As we drank our coffee I asked if they were going home by way of South Dakota or taking the northern route through North Dakota.

"Neither," said Linda. "We are going over the Cooke City highway, through Yellowstone Park and home."

"You've got to be kidding," I said. "Ohio is still east of us, isn't it?"

She laughed, "Yes, but we just cannot miss seeing those mountains and that beautiful scenery one more time. So we are going home that way."

I shook my head. "You will enjoy the park. It just seems funny to go west to go east!" I guess they had good reason.

I thought about it later and laughed again. I decided to send them a road map with red lines drawn all over it on optional ways to get from Colstrip to Ohio for future reference.

But a spiritual comparison came to my mind. (It usually does when I am judgmental about someone else's actions!) I thought about how many times Procrastination has used her power to make me take the long way around. Putting off doing some task until I am under pressure, in a hurry and suffering the consequences of being unprepared.

I take the "long way around" in doing household tasks. I'll start out to clean the kitchen, take a dirty towel to the laundry room, sort some clothes and take a load of clean clothes to the bedroom. As I walk by the freezer I take some meat out for dinner and get back to the kitchen forty-five minutes later. Time-consultants tell us that sticking to a task until it is completed is the most efficient use of our time.

God tells us in His Word to pray without ceasing. Jesus spent many early morning hours in prayer. He commanded us to pray. I have read the biographies of many spiritual giants and the busier their day was to be, the earlier they arose for prayer and devotions. God wants us to talk to Him. The older I get, the more I see how much more is accomplished on the days I schedule time with the Lord first. Some days I get in a rush with all I have to do and plan to pray later. I think that is what you could call taking the long way around.

That map that had the zigzag lines going from Colstrip to Ohio was really funny when I was doing it. It is not quite so funny today. I think I saw myself there.

Read
Luke 5:1-16; Mark 1:35; 6:46

My prayer of joy for today:

The Other Brake Pedal

I traveled south a few weeks ago for some speaking engage-ments. My friend Phyllis went with me. We drove through a snowstorm coming home and hit some icy roads. Phyllis never once shouted, "Watch out! You're going into the ditch!" She never asked me if I realized how icy the roads were or questioned the speed I was driving. And I didn't tell her how to drive either. I didn't grab the door handle in fear when the car slid a bit. I didn't tell her there was a better way to drive to the motel. And I know why we didn't.

Because we are not married to each other. Isn't it interest-ing that when a couple is dating, they sit close together and driving is simply a means to get from one place to another? But let the rings be on the fingers and a few months of mar-ried life be behind the loving couple and driving changes from the "means" to a call to arms. How a man can go from a driver as skillful as Jeff Gordon to a totally incompetent risk to other motorists just by saying "I do" baffles me. And how a woman can be given the keys to a prized sports car as a sign of ever-lasting love before the wedding and become a hazard going to the grocery store later is a puzzle.

Just listen to the couple discussing a trip: *"He* got us lost." *"She* took the wrong turn." *"He* drove like a maniac." *"She* drove like an idiot."

Robert and I have had our share of driving discussions. I put a dent in the floorboard of our car going down a mountainside in Idaho. I had the brakes on the whole way down, and I wasn't even driving. And he headed for the floor when he thought I was going to cause a six-car pileup in Dallas. We got so lost in Los Angeles looking for Marineland once that we had to stop and get gas again . . . and barely stayed married!

There are some solutions. Monitor your reactions when someone else is driving. Are you nervous then, or is it just with your mate? That would focus attention on the possible source of the problem. Remind yourself that this woman or this man loves you. They would not try to hurt you. Put some faith into practice. Talk over your fears with each other (but not in the car). Discuss driving when you are in a good frame of mind. Do not allow the words "always" and "never" in your conversation. And try this: Tape a note in your car that says, "Do to others as you would have them do to you" (Luke 6:31). Not only will this help the problem, it will improve your driving manners as well.

Read
John 16

My prayer of joy for today:

Day 27

The Lost Coin

Mom and I were sitting in a booth at Martin's Café. Dad had taken the stock truck to Bozeman, hoping to buy some yearlings. We were enjoying a bowl of tasty bean soup and a cup of coffee.

Our friend, Shirley, was cleaning up tables after the noon rush. "You know, a quarter isn't worth much these days," she said. "I was at the post office this morning. There was a quarter on the floor and nobody would pick it up."

"Well, did you pick it up?" Mom asked.

"No, it was right by the door. I thought if I bent over to pick it up, I'd get banged on the head by the door. It was only a quarter."

Mr. and Mrs. Wood were sitting at a table near us. "I would have picked it up, even if it was a penny," she said.

"That's just good exercise," said my mom. " 'Course they say, as you get older, you ought to check around on the floor and see if there is anything else to do there while you're down." We laughed.

Mrs. Woods added the final quip, "Well, I'd have a lot of time to look. If I bend down, I might just as well spend the day!"

Dear Lord, please help me to have a good attitude about getting older! I want to have a sweet spirit, inner peace, content-

ment and still be a light for You. It sure is hard to have much of a testimony when one is a grouch. It is not much fun for the grouch either. Lord, could You please fill my cup of joy often, even when I get so old I forget where I put the cup? Amen.

Read
Psalm 71

My prayer of joy for today:

Day 28

Greeting at the Well

The woman was scorned by the people in her town. She was looked down on by those around her. She was used to being ignored. Then she met Jesus.

> Now Jacob's well was there. Jesus therefore, being wearied with his journey, sat thus on the well: and it was about the sixth hour. There cometh a woman of Samaria to draw water: Jesus saith unto her, Give me to drink. (For his disciples were gone away unto the city to buy meat.) Then saith the woman of Samaria unto him, How is it that thou, being a Jew, askest drink of me, which am a woman of Samaria? for the Jews have no dealings with the Samaritans. (John 4:6-9, KJV)

It was not the normal thing for Jews to speak to Samaritans. Ridicule and rebuff were accepted behavior—so much so that the Samaritans had come to expect it. This woman not only expected to be ignored by the Jews, she expected scorn from the townsfolk as well. She had learned to go to the well when the other women wouldn't be there. Put yourself at the scene. Think of her thoughts when she saw someone was at the well. Did she think about turning around and going home? Did she grit her teeth and decide to tough it out?

Picture Jesus sitting there. Jesus, who knew everything about her—and loved her. Speaking to her was not a gesture of pity. We have learned that Jesus was not a "respecter of persons." There was no prejudice on His part. It is the *inside* that is important to Him.

> Whose adorning let it not be that outward adorning of plaiting the hair, and of wearing of gold, or of putting on of apparel; *but let it be the hidden man of the heart,* in that which is not corruptible, even the ornament of a meek and quiet spirit, *which is in the sight of God of great price.* (1 Peter 3:3-4, KJV, emphasis added).

I believe God put this encounter in His Word so that we might learn. Do we model Jesus' behavior at the well? At the well—of work? In the grocery store? We spend so much time and energy on what does not matter. We know the Source of Living Water. Let that be the motivation of our conversations with the townsfolk around us. Bring an offering of inner joy to others, especially to those who are unaccustomed to friendship. You will be amazed at how God uses your willingness to love others! He can use us to bring townsfolk to Him. In that way, we will have joy overflowing in our own cup as well.

Read
John 4:1-42

My prayer of joy for today:

Day 29

Me and the YWCA

Do children ever fully appreciate all the sacrifices that their parents make for them? I hope that one of my children will read this and nominate me for "Mother of the Decade," because I joined the local YWCA only on their behalf. I got worried about them falling into a river or lake—because I wouldn't be able to save them due to my lack of swimming ability. It took more courage then you can imagine (note that, boys) to sign up for the Beginners' Water Exercise Class.

I managed to find my way through the maze of halls and doors to the proper dressing room. I got into my suit. (Oh, my suit. I bought it in 1976 in the midst of the bicentennial excitement. It is red, white and blue and it was a hit that year. Since then, I feel like a flag when I wear it.)

I walked from the locker room. I had to leave my glasses in the locker. I can barely distinguish shapes without them. That added to my discomfort. I kept my nose on the blue arrows that said "POOL" along the hall. When I saw a wide expanse of aqua space, I was sure I had arrived at the exercise class.

After a few minutes of squinting scrutiny, I saw that the women were swimming laps back and forth in the pool. I proceeded confidently down to the deep end and jumped in, swimming my best to the other end. I made a rather Olympic style turn and proceeded back. I had gone about eight feet when I swam right into a lady. "Oops," I blubbered. "Sorry." I got my body back into fish position and started again, only to run head-on into another lady. "Sorry," I gasped. This stopping and starting was playing me out. The third swimmer in my line of attack saw me coming and made a detour.

The fourth woman paused, treading water, and yelled, "We swim *up* the outside of the pool and we swim *back* in the middle of the pool!" I had been going down that pool like a bowling ball knocking pins right and left. I quickly swam to the edge and got out of the pool.

I made my way to the locker room. I got my clothes and my glasses back on. I went straight from the YWCA to the Dairy Queen. There is only so much sacrificing a mother can do before she has to recharge her batteries!

Read
John 5:1-23

My prayer of joy for today:

Day 30

Too Good to Be True

There is a miracle happening at our house. Well, it is going to happen. I have purchased new computer software. It is a complete recipe management program. Of course I have cookbooks and a drawer filled with recipes. They mostly flopped. This is different. This program is even going to save us money. The box says you can select recipes and then prepare detailed shopping lists.

The feature I think I will like best is called "refrigerator search." If you can't decide what to have for dinner, the manual says you can use the feature to find recipes that use the groceries you have. The instructions say to list your refrigerator contents in the blinking boxes viewed on the screen. I like the line that says you can prepare "delicious meals" with the ingredients you have on hand. Robert has been waiting a long time for a delicious meal. He did comment after reading the brochure, "You mean that if you enter wilted lettuce, sour milk, shriveled dry beans and a clump of hamburger that is turning yellow in an old margarine tub into those blinking boxes on the screen, we will get a delicious meal?"

"Yup," I said smugly. "That's all there is to it. Wait until you see this."

He stood there in amazement. (I *think* that is what it was.)

I went to the computer and followed the directions to install this miraculous invention. I didn't quite understand the "right click for mouse menus." I don't particularly plan on feeding any mice. But I followed the directions and loaded the program. "Reboot your computer and then double click on the Recipes icon." I did that. It wouldn't work. I tried over and over. Nothing would work. I sat there staring at the screen.

Did I get angry? No. Did I get frustrated? No. Discouraged? Not a chance. As a matter of fact I started to smile. "Well, thanks, Lord, for this little blessing. I feel better about myself already." If this computer with its 635,427,920 bytes of memory doesn't have enough brain power to comprehend all this cooking stuff, it is no wonder that I can't master the subject! I shut the computer off and put the disc back in the box—joyfully!

"Hey, Robert, want to go to the Coal Bowl for supper?"

Read
Exodus 16

My prayer of joy for today:

Day 31

It's Hot Down There

R obert had a conference in Dallas, Texas, several years ago. I went along since there were activities for the spouses too. We were with people from all over the country. I had been telling them that it had been 35 degrees when we left Colstrip to come to Texas. We had spent a stifling day on the tour bus seeing the sights when, as we were driving down the street, I saw one of those digital blinking signs that show time and temperature.

I couldn't believe what I saw. I turned to Audrey from New Jersey, who was sitting beside me, and said, "No wonder we're so hot. It's 99.6."

She said, "Oh, I thought it was hot, but I didn't think it was that hot."

Then the bus pulled up to the intersection. As we rounded the corner I realized that it was a gas station. "99.6" was the price of the gas! We didn't have digital gas signs in Montana then. I kept quiet after that.

There is a time to be quiet—and a time to speak. Being quiet about the heat is not always right. The old hellfire and damnation preachers scared everyone so badly that for many years conscientious Christians have not dared to say the word "hell." Yet people need to know that indeed there is a choice to be made concerning eternity.

> And I saw the dead, small and great, stand before God; and the books were opened: and another book was opened, which is the book of life. . . . And whosoever was not found written in the book of life was cast into the lake of fire. (Revelation 20:12, 15, KJV)

Rosebud Creek rancher Wally McRae, a world-renowned colorful cowboy poet, was in the hospital in Billings. I went to see him on my way to speak to a ladies' conference. After we visited, I said that I had better get going to my meeting. His parting words were, "Well, give 'em hell." I laughed . . . until I got to my car. Then I cried. Because he spoke words of truth and vision, whether he knew it or not. There is a choice. Don't be quiet.

Read
Revelation 20

My prayer of joy for today:

Day 32

Waiting

We have dear friends who are waiting for their third baby to be born in the next few days. They have two boys. Is this next baby going to be a girl or another boy? Is today the day? What if there is a snowstorm and the roads drift over? Waiting . . .

Another friend's dad is dying with cancer. They have done all the medical treatment they can do. He is in a California hospital. His son and his family live in Montana. Every time the phone rings they wonder what the message will be. Should they go now? Should they make plans for tomorrow? What about next week? Waiting . . .

There is more. A friend had not heard from her son in another state for almost four weeks. Their last phone conversation was filled with fear and discouragement. She has been praying and waiting . . .

A letter from a friend told of marriage difficulties. Finally she issued an ultimatum—make a decision: stay or go. My friend is praying. And waiting . . .

Life is full of waiting. These are just a few instances that I know about. There are those among you waiting for that job offer, waiting for graduation, waiting for that letter. How do we wait in these difficult situations when we have done all we can do and yet the situation goes on? I don't have all the answers. I don't like to wait either. Yet I know where I have found strength. Strength and hope and patience. That is in God's Word, the Bible. What comfort our Lord can give us in time of need! This is not just my idea. God says, "For everything that was written in the past was written to teach us, so that through endurance and the encouragement of the Scriptures we might have hope" (Romans 15:4).

We have choices about how we act and react during waiting. We can stew and worry and sweat and pace and make ourselves and everyone around us miserable. Or we can pray patiently with hope and assurance that God does hear our prayers. The Bible says so.

Several of us joined that mother in prayer Wednesday night for that son. He called late that night. Coincidence? I don't think so. The friend with marriage difficulties wrote this week, "He is staying. We are going to work at our marriage."

If you are going through a waiting time right now, get your Bible out and read Psalm 145. You can gain hope from God's Word. That is a promise. Also, call a friend or two and have them pray with you. They can walk through the waiting time with you. I have a verse taped to the wall above this desk. It says, "The LORD is good unto them that wait for him, to the soul that seeketh him" (Lamentations 3:25. KJV). That helps me in waiting times.

Read
Isaiah 40:28-31

My prayer of joy for today:

68

Day 33

A Puddle of Joy

ƆOY HINGE PIN

*"Weeping may endure for a night,
but joy cometh in the morning." (Psalm 30:5, KJV)*

Grandma used to tell me, "A good cry does you good." She was right. Crying is not wrong. Tears are the outward sign of inner sadness. It would be a mighty cold world if God did not create us with emotions. David wept. He cried his eyes out: "I am weary with my groaning; all the night make I my bed to swim; I water my couch with my tears" (Psalm 6:6, KJV). Jesus wept. *But we have a promise* that He will wipe away all tears when we get to heaven. It will be a time of praise and rejoicing.

Here on earth there are reasons to cry—lots of them! If we just think about the lost souls, unloved children and empty lives without hope, we can dissolve into a puddle of tears for a week. When we lose a loved one, grief rips out part of our heart. We could cry forever. That is where my joy flows deep. I know that God understands!

I don't hear God saying, "Straighten up! Get a grip! Stop that bawlin'! Pick yourself up by your bootstraps and get on with your life!"

No. God, my loving heavenly Father, says, "I, God Almighty, will wipe away your tears. I will turn your mourning into joy. I will cause the widow's heart to sing for joy" (see Revelation 7:17; Isaiah 61:3; Job 29:13).

He comes in lovingkindness, understanding our sorrows and tears. He does not despise our tears. He takes them and changes them into joy. That is His promise. "For I will turn their mourning into joy, and will comfort them, and make them rejoice from their sorrow" (Jeremiah 31:13, KJV).

I sit in a puddle of tears and *God, according to His Word, lovingly wipes them away, and sets me back down without condemnation in a puddle of joy!* Therein lies another hinge pin of my joy. Praise God!

**Read
Psalm 56**

My prayer of joy for today:

Day 34

Hot Little Red Bug

Dear Newspaper Editor:

I was so surprised to read in the police report in your newspaper that my illustrious little red VW Bug had caught fire because (to quote your report) "pan of ashes set on engine caught fire" at 7433 Castle Rock Lake Drive.

It was nine degrees below that morning when the driver went out and started the Bug to let it warm up. When the passenger went out to get in, he saw the Bug was warm. Very warm. Flames were shooting from underneath and out the back.

He yelled, "Call the fire department!"

The driver got out, rather quickly, of course, and started throwing snow on the fire. I called the fire department. The passenger ran to the garage to get a bucket. We had two buckets sitting by the garage door. One holds ashes (long cold) in case of ice on our driveway. He grabbed that bucket and raced back to the fire. When the fire department, fire trucks, sheriff's deputy, patrolman and several others arrived in response to the alarm, the Bug fire was out. We saw immediately that a small gas line had ruptured, spraying gas on the engine and of course igniting the fire. I am glad they responded quickly. There was a chance of an explosion.

However, after reading the published report in your newspaper, I am glad the passenger did not grab the other bucket in the garage. It holds the kitty litter for oil spills on the driveway. Then the report might have read, "Pan of kitty litter set on engine caught fire."

The Bug has a colorful history. I went to Billings to buy drapes, but bought the Bug instead. Surprised my family. Then, the first time I went to put gas in it, I opened the trunk, the hood, the glove compartment—everything—looking for the hidden gas tank spout. With a kind gentleman's help, I finally found it. It took fourteen cents worth of gas (the gas gauge is broken). It is sure economical.

So now there is another chapter in its history. One friend thought it was a unique idea, having a hot little red bug to drive. "You could melt the icy streets as you drive along," he said. Now I just tell people, "Oh yes, to warm it up, we just put cold ashes in a plastic ice cream bucket on the engine. Starts it right up!"

Thanks for a good chuckle,
Lois Olmstead

PS: I have a Bug for sale. Slightly heated, awfully cheap!

Read
1 Kings 18

My prayer of joy for today:

The Rest of the Story

M ost people have heard the story from the Bible of the three men in the fiery furnace. If it were a game show question, you might even be able to name them. The answer is Shadrach, Meshach and Abednego. And surely you have heard the story of Daniel in the lions' den?

However, not many people have heard the rest of the story. They have heard the end—but not the beginning. It is recorded in the first chapter of the book of Daniel in the Old Testament. The Babylonians and King Nebuchadnezzar conquered Jerusalem. The king ordered his men to bring up some of the children of the Israelites. He wanted some with "no blemish, but well favoured, and skilful in all wisdom, and cunning in knowledge, and understanding science" (Daniel 1:4, KJV). In other words, the cream of the crop. The king gave them a special diet to follow. After three years they were to stand before the king.

"But Daniel purposed in his heart that he would not defile himself with . . . the king's meat, nor with the wine which he drank" (1:8, KJV). The man who had been put in charge of these young lads was fearful of the king. "If you are worse than the others, you will endanger my head," he told Daniel (see 1:10).

Daniel told him to run a test. "Give the four of us just vegetables and water for ten days and then compare us with the others" (see 1:12-13). This they did. In ten days, their countenances were fairer and fatter than all the others. The Bible tells us, "As for these four children, God gave them knowledge and skill in all learning and wisdom" (1:17, KJV). At the end of the set time, all the young men were brought before the king. None was found like Daniel, Shadrach, Meshach and Abednego. The Bible goes on to say that the king sought their advice in all matters of wisdom and understanding. You can read the rest of the story in Daniel to review the episode of the fiery furnace and the lions' den and how God used these young men for His glory.

Daniel 1:8 is underlined in my Bible. I like that verse: "Daniel purposed in his heart . . ." (KJV). We can set our minds and our will to follow the Lord. We can set our goals in line with the Word of God. No, I haven't had to struggle with eating the king's meat and drinking the king's wine, but I have struggled with finding time for devotions. With finding time for Bible reading and prayer. With being faithful to helping others. There can be struggles with saying kind things or thinking pure thoughts.

At those times I think of Daniel, then I set my own will. I "purpose in my heart to have devotions first thing early in the morning." Or I "purpose in my heart to think only kind thoughts this day." And I am reminded again that God honored them for following Him by giving them wisdom and understanding.

That is enough for me.

Read
Daniel 1

My prayer of joy for today:

Day 36

The Mouse

The experts say a person really has to hit bottom and realize he has a problem before a behavior can be changed. I have hit rock bottom. I am so miserable I may need counseling about this cooking thing. My rapid descent to utter despair started with a mouse. I came out of our bedroom shortly before dawn last Friday. I was dressed and ready for my devotions and coffee. I heard a noise. *Scritch, scritch, munch, scritch* went the noise.

Drats! I bet we have a mouse! Here in my kitchen somewhere, I have Scritch Toes! "Oh, good grief! Robert, get up! There is a mouse right on the kitchen counter!" Since I was yelling, he got up. The mouse left his dining beside the toaster and zipped down one of the burners on the stove.

"Grab a newspaper," said Robert. We both got into position on each side of the stove. One by one we removed the burners and the drip pans. Then Robert hit the stove. The mouse did not come out from the top of the stove. Instead, Scritch came flying out the bottom. He ran over Robert's toes and headed straight for the corner cupboard. With a small jump, he disappeared. We threw open every cupboard door. The mouse was gone. With major whining about having to empty all the cupboards and washing all the stuff in Purex, I left for work. No time for devotions. God knew the mood I was in anyway. When I went out the door, Robert was putting cheese in the mouse trap.

Saturday morning I got up thinking, *Bite the bullet, Lois. Just do it.* I got the Lysol, donned rubber gloves and opened all the cupboards. No mouse tracks. I looked under the sink. No mouse tracks. I pulled out all the drawers. No mouse tracks. No way to get in or out. Stumped, I decided to follow his trail. Under the corner cupboard, I found a small opening under the cupboard flooring. Hallelujah! At least he was under the cupboards, not in them. I stuffed the hole with steel wool, saying, "Farewell, Scritch. You are unwelcome in this house."

Then I tackled the decontamination phase. I took everything off the cupboards, sanitizing as I went. I found a colorful trail of cookie sprinkles. The trail went from the plate of Easter cookies I had left on the counter, around the sink, past the toaster to the stove. I disinfected everything. Then the stove. The burners and pans were still off. I grabbed my rag—and one look told me where Scritch had set up housekeeping—in my stovetop, under the burners! Tracks were plentiful. The evidence was plain.

I fell into a basketful of depression as I cleaned the stove. *Lois, you are the only woman in America who could have a motel for a mouse in her stove. Every other woman cooks on her stove!*

Is there a group for non-cooking homemakers? I am ready. I *know* I have a problem!

Read
Isaiah 66 (KJV)

My prayer of joy for today:

Day 37

More Than One Card

In going through files this week, I found a card from Phyllis that she sent after I learned that I had cancer. The verse on the card was good.

No matter how steep the hill or the mountain is,
The Lord is going to climb it with you!

The note she wrote on the back was enlightening.

"Dear Lois, I'm sorry. I didn't know this was a three-card illness until you told me about the three cards Micki had sent. So I guess I better catch up. I suppose Micki's sent four by now," she wrote. Then the note went on, "I guess I have always just been a one-card-illness person but this sure opened up a Pandora's box on cards. I found some neat ones! However, if you should run out of illness before I run out of cards, don't worry. I'll just send them to myself on bad days. Love, Phyllis."

We have laughed about this together since. Yet it taught a very important lesson that has had an impact on both of us since that time. In bearing one another's burdens, we all do the things that will let that one know we are thinking of them and praying for them. Yet through my cancer experience I was blessed by the number of people who sent more than one card. Several people sent cards every few weeks as I went through treatment. And some sent cards to Robert as well. We were touched deeply by this thoughtfulness.

I thought I should just pass it on. There are many more-than-one-card troubles in the world around us. We should probably include more-than-one-phone call, more-than-one-meal and more-than-one-visit in that file as well!

Read
Psalm 34

My prayer of joy for today:

Cleaning and Confessing

It was my annual January housecleaning spree. Everything was out of the living room and dining room. All the pictures off the wall, all the knickknacks set aside and all the books out of the bookcases. I took the curtains down and washed them. Even the mini-blinds did not escape my tidiness attack. When I had that done, I cleaned and painted all the walls. Then the carpet shampooers were called.

I could not believe how much dirt I found. In my defense, the dirt was not showing. It was hidden behind, underneath, in between and back of everything! Some of those pesky gnats from summer evenings past had even found their way between the glass and the print in a framed picture.

I cringed—and went into a sneezing fit when I took my curtains down. I had no idea that much dust had accumulated. The mini-blinds left a muddy ring in my tub when I gave them a bath. And the bookcases . . . !

As usual, it seems I get my most significant spiritual lessons from my everyday life. This is no exception. Sometimes I don't realize that I am in need of a good cleaning—spiritually. Sin creeps in just like those tiny gnats. Like my dust. It may not even be noticeable to a casual observer. And just like my dust, if not taken care of on a regular basis, it builds up: a little anger there, a touch of selfishness here and in a corner some envy or lying.

You know, the last few weeks, when my dirty house started really getting to me, I was reluctant to have people over. I knew my house needed a good cleaning. This is true with my spiritual life as well. I let these sinful attitudes go until (all of a sudden?) I realize I am feeling out of sorts. My praying and Bible reading times become cool. I don't much want to be around people.

I am so thankful that God is in the cleansing business. He says, "If we confess our sins, he is faithful and just to forgive us our sins, and to cleanse us from all unrighteousness" (1 John 1:9, KJV).

Now I am in the process of putting things back in my clean rooms. I made a rule for myself: Nothing could go back that was not polished, waxed, washed or dusted. What a thrill to sit relaxed in my chair and know that my home is cleaned inside and inside the inside. It feels even better when I do the same with the inside of me. After some time alone with God, confessing and repenting, followed by thanksgiving and praise, I feel clean on the inside too. "Oh, the joy and peace of cleanliness," I said to me. I feel a nap coming on.

Read
Ezekiel 36:21-38

My prayer of joy for today:

The Kidnap Kaper

"This year during the holidays we are going to invite several groups over," she says. They didn't.

"Let's go to the city one weekend and see all the art galleries," he says. They didn't.

"If we have one couple from church over every week, we could get to know the new people," she says. They didn't.

"Let's plan a party night with the kids every other week. One night can be a circus night, one night a picnic, one night a country fair," the committee said. They didn't.

Good intentions. Ways to make mundane days special. Ways to make precious memories. We just don't do it!

Not so the ladies from the First Baptist Church in Colstrip. They scheduled a brunch for the ladies in our community at 10:30 on Saturday morning at their church. But they didn't tell everyone they'd be picking them up—early in the morning! The first clue something was up (most of the ladies weren't!) was a yellow school bus honking in the driveway. Then furious pounding on the front door. "Get your shoes and your coat," I was told. "You are being kidnaped!"

I didn't feel out of place in my robe and duck slippers when I got on the bus. The passengers were in short nightgowns and long ones. There were sleep shirts and sweats. (What were you wearing at 7 a.m. last Saturday morning?) My only regret was not grabbing my coffee when I was escorted from my house. After we had bumped and backed and bounced through the streets of Colstrip for two hours picking up other unsuspecting sleepy people, I would have paid $10 for a cup of coffee.

The "Kidnap Kaper" was hilarious and fun. We found out where people lived. We met new folks. The best part was the sumptuous breakfast waiting for us when we disembarked at the church. We found out husbands and daddies had been privy to the joyful surprise.

"Wouldn't it be a fun idea to have a Come-As-You-Are party? We could invite different ladies in town. We could surprise them by getting them out of bed on Saturday morning!" they said. *And they did!*

Read
Matthew 21:38-31

My prayer of joy for today:

Day 40

Runner's Wall

"It's called runner's wall," Dennis Limberhand told me. He was relating how marathon runners will come up against a place where they feel they cannot run another step. "It can hit at the nineteen-mile mark or the twenty-two-mile mark. You just don't know when it is going to rise up in front of you," Dennis explained. "It is the worst pain you can imagine. Your body does not want to go on."

"What do you do? How do you make yourself go on?" I asked.

"You just know you have to run through it."

"I feel there is a very important parable coming here," I told Dennis. "I like the phrase 'run through it.' It gives you the optimistic goal of doing it! There is hope. That wall could relate to many different problems we face. I'm going to have to ponder this awhile."

And I have. In relation to my procrastination, to healthy eating, to exercise, to devotions, prayer. . . . The list would be different for each one of us. To some it would mean breaking a habit that is harmful. To another it would be housework, schoolwork or maybe being a couch potato in front of the television.

Kelly Cole has won many races in our state. In response to my question about runners' wall, she said, "Oh yes, I remem--

ber the first time I ran into it. I was running fine, feeling great. Then at eighteen miles I turned cold. I felt I could not run another step. That feeling stayed with me for three or four miles."

"How did you keep going?"

"I just kept thinking of other things. I played mind games with myself. I just ran through it. Being able to finish what I have started in running has helped me to get through other difficult things."

Debbie Vetsch is another gal I see out running. "Even when you think you can't, you just give it another push. One more step," she said, "and then you can. You break through the wall."

There is hope. The wall looms in front of us, but it only has a certain depth. Run through it: there is another side—the victory side. I think I even see the finish line. I think I can hear the crowd cheering as they see us coming . . . through the wall! Thanks, Dennis, Kelly and Debbie. We are going to be running through right along with you—with joy.

Read
1 Corinthians 9:24-27

My prayer of joy for today:

Day 41

The Cattle Rustler

First of all, it was a three-day cattle drive. But if you consider the day I spent in my basement looking for my long-lost cowboy hat, boots and Levis . . . and the two days after the trail drive that I sat on a heating pad recuperating—it was actually a six-day experience!

Trailing the herd of 275 cows and calves through the beautiful, scenic Shields Valley for forty miles was a real treat. We got off our horses and walked some to keep the saddle sores to a minimum. My dad, the trail boss, said we would have to spend the night out with the cattle. We had six people with six down-filled sleeping bags, two air mattresses and a good amount of cow punching gear in the two-person tent. When one person turned, we all had to adjust. The first night out it rained. We woke up soggy and sore.

Two hundred and seventy-five mothers and children are hard to keep together, be they cows or people. I had the job of making sure none of the stragglers were left behind. It was slow going at the tail of the drive. We were walking our horses when we saw children by the fence near a house up the road. They were yelling and waving. That fed my prideful vanity of being a real cowpoke. Right inside the fence line, which was partially falling down, I spied a cow, evidently a straggler trying to hide from our wary eyes.

I rode up like John Wayne, hollering, "Get out of the way!" The kids thought I was yelling at them. They ran and so did the cow. They ran to the house and the cow ran to join the rest of the herd.

Seven hours and twenty-one minutes later, the cow's owner came to claim our 276th cow—the one that I had so proudly rounded up! He asked my dad if he had just "happened to pick up any strays along the way." Shortly thereafter he found his cow.

Spurs, bowlegs and cattle rustling are not really my line. I decided that about two minutes after the cow jumped into the man's trailer and he waved to me with a smile as he left. I think I will stick to writing.

I just have twelve more miles with this herd before I can go home. I am no longer bringing up the stragglers in the rear. The trail boss wants me to ride beside him.

Read
Psalm 50

My prayer of joy for today:

The Comforter Has Come

ƆOY ҤINGE ꝐIN

*"But the Comforter, which is the Holy Ghost,
whom the Father will send in my name, he shall teach you
all things, and bring all things to your remembrance,
whatsoever I have said unto you. Peace I leave with you,
my peace I give unto you: not as the world giveth,
give I unto you. Let not your heart be troubled, neither
let it be afraid. Ye have heard how I said unto you,
I go away, and come again unto you. If ye loved me,
ye would rejoice." (John 14:26-28, KJV)*

Stand on the hillside near Bethany amongst the other people. John and Simon Peter are standing there and so are
Matthew and Luke. The two Marys are there. Andrew and
Philip and Thomas are there. Can you feel the excitement in
the air? You can just feel something important is about to
happen. You are still in shock over the events of the last few
weeks. The crucifixion. The resurrection! Jesus here walking
and teaching among us again. Now He is standing at the top
of this hill. His arms are raised. There is a heavenly glow
about Him. He gazes at each one with a look of tremendous

love that touches our very souls. Love that is *agape* love, perfect love, love cradled in grace and mercy. We stand with arms at our sides, heads lifted toward Him and ears tuned to hear every word.

Then He speaks again. He is leaving. A cloud of love is sent from heaven to escort Him—the Son of God—home. He says, "Wait here. When I get to my Father, I will send the Holy Ghost to come upon you." Two angels stand where He stood. They speak of His coming again.

I love the way these folks left the hillside. Sorrowful? Angry? No. Dear friends, get this: "And it came to pass, while he blessed them, he was parted from them, and carried up into heaven. And they worshipped him, and returned to Jerusalem with great joy: And were continually in the temple, praising and blessing God. Amen" (Luke 24:51-53, KJV).

Jesus had said He would not leave us comfortless. He did not leave us alone. We know He does what He says He will do. After all, He defeated death. He is our Healer and Savior and Coming King. Therein lies joy. A joy hinge pin is that *the Comforter has come.* Tarry on the hillside a little longer. Raise your arms. Thank God for the Holy Ghost. Let His love fill your being. You are loved and you are not alone.

Read
John 14:16-21; 16:7-14

My prayer of joy for today:

Day 43

Lisa's Gift

A gift I will never forget was given to me several years ago. I was taking ceramic classes at a local shop. Lots of fun gals were in the weekly classes, including my new daughter-in-law, Lisa, and her mother.

I had vocalized several times how much I hated the poured-out, lookalike, awful-shaped kitchen sets. You could get napkin holders, scrubby-holders, canisters, salt and pepper shakers and spoon racks all to match. Now don't be offended if you happen to have one of these sets. I am sure they look lovely. It was just that in my blue kitchen with old antique kitchenware on display, the lime-green, cutesy, aproned, doll-faced doughgirl stuff would not fit.

"A set like that would be so far down on my gift list," I quipped more than once, "that it wouldn't even show up!"

Well, close to Christmas, Thelma, the owner of the shop, had a party. We had all become such good friends we decided to have a gift exchange and drew names. The night of the party we took turns opening our gifts. I was surprised and delighted to see that Lisa had drawn my name when I opened the card on my beautifully wrapped gift. As I was getting ready to open it she said, "I have to tell you that I didn't get it all done. But I am planning on finishing the rest for you later."

"Oh-h-h-h-h-h, oh-h-h-h-h-h," I said as I opened it. And I just kept saying it over and over. I didn't know what to do . . . or say. "Oh-h-h-h-h." There in the tissue paper was a napkin holder. Lime-green doll face, apron and all. And a soap dish. And a spoon holder.

I started to giggle—this had to be a joke. I looked at Lisa and her mom and everyone else. They were all just smiling and saying, "Oh, how nice."

Maybe it isn't a joke, I thought. "Oh-h-h-h-h."

I had what seemed like hours of intense anxiety before they finally erupted into peals of laughter. And though I never want to go through trying to figure out how to say something nice about something I didn't want from someone I love, I will never forget the gift.

Knowing that Lisa felt good enough about our relationship as daughter-in-law and mother-in-law that she could pull such a joke was a treasure—and the best gift of all. (And no, I didn't keep the lime-green stuff, and Lisa said that was OK!)

Read
Psalm 100

My prayer of joy for today:

Through the Storm

I was scheduled to speak at a ladies' retreat at Mountain Top Retreat Center. The lodge and cabins perch on a mountain off Cottonwood Canyon near Bozeman. It is a beautiful site. The day before I was to leave, snow began falling. It didn't let up. It snowed all night.

I called the chairman. "Well, it's snowing hard here," she said, "but we still plan on going. No one has canceled."

Over a foot of snow was on the ground the next morning. The radio was broadcasting road reports and none of them sounded good. Calls between the chairman and myself were filled with indecision and commitments to more prayer. I had struggled with my topic for this retreat. At one point I was berating myself for accepting the invitation. I was feeling more inadequate than usual. "What words of wisdom could I possibly give to help someone?" I was a few hours away from my first spot on the program and nothing had jelled. "Maybe God knew I was going to be snowed in and wasn't going to be the speaker anyway," I said.

Finally I had to just yield. "OK, Lord. I trust You. We will start out. You direct. If the roads are too bad, we will turn back. Either way, I am available to speak or not speak, as You direct."

It looked terrible as we backed out of our driveway. Robert was driving. I had my notebook and Bible on my lap so I could work on my notes on the way. We got about twelve miles from home. "It isn't as bad here, is it?" Robert commented. And it wasn't. We soon were out of the brunt of the storm. The roads were barely wet. I breathed a prayer, "OK, Lord," and began going over some notes. He drove and I wrote. The way soon was clear—both the roadway and my direction. I was to speak three times and the three topics became clear and concise. Three hours later I was ready to give the ladies what the Lord had given me. I closed my notebook.

The roads were good until we got outside Bozeman. Robert unloaded my suitcase at the bottom of the mountain. I bundled up and grabbed my notes. A four-wheel drive van shuttled me and my stuff to Mountain Top. It was beautiful. There were fifty-five inches of snow at the lodge. The retreat was an awesome blessing from start to finish. Over and over we commented, "What a loss if we had canceled our time together!" I thought about the storm at home and the storm at my destination. I thought about the clear sailing in between and the blessings we would have missed. . . . I think I feel a lesson coming on for my next retreat!

Read
Mark 4

My prayer of joy for today:

Day 45

Todd's Sweatshirts

We all went into the discount store and headed different directions. Todd stopped at the sweatshirts. Snowmobile season was coming soon. A huge yellow sign announced, "THREE FOR $10." This was good. He didn't need any help from his wife. He proudly picked three. We all met back at the pickup. Todd had his treasures in one hand. In the other hand he had the sales receipt. He was miffed. "I found a sale on sweatshirts," he said, "but they charged me full price! I'm going in there and getting my money back."

He walked as a man with a purpose. His back was ramrod straight as he marched through the double doors. His mission took about fifteen minutes. His second trip out the door with his sweatshirts was that of a beaten man. "I marched right up to the clerk and told her I had been charged the wrong price. She bellowed, 'PRICE CHECK, NUMBER FIVE!' over the intercom. I had everyone's attention. The sweatshirt person came over. He said the sale sign is for the underwear on the top shelf. With victory all over her face, the clerk asked me if I still wanted the sweatshirts. I couldn't let them think I was cheap. I've got my own job. I've got my own checkbook. Now I have three sweatshirts for $21." We laughed as he related the story. "And every time I wear one, I'll remember feeling like an idiot too!"

But the last laugh was yet to come. It seems the weather cooled. Todd decided he'd wear one of his new sweatshirts to work. He grabbed the blue one from the closet and swung it over his head with his arms in the sleeves.

He got stuck! Now he was a desperate man—he couldn't get caught because we had teased him unmercifully. But he couldn't get unstuck either. Of course Lisa walked in just then. With great amusement, she got him freed. They checked the tag, and sure enough, it was a large. A boy's large.

A few days after this column appeared in the local newspaper, Todd was at work at the steam-generating plants. A voice came over the paging system for the 750 employees. "Attention, Todd Olmstead. There is a sweatshirt sale in aisle 13 by the cooling towers!"

This shows what a wonderful Christian man he has grown up to be. He forgave me!

Read
Psalm 19

My prayer of joy for today:

Day 46

Starve a Cold

I get so mixed up. Is that old adage "Starve a cold and feed a fever?" Or is it "Feed a cold and starve a fever?" I do know two things as I emerge from a tunnel of sick. I am emerging with four new pounds of fat attached to my body because I couldn't remember what the adage was. So I fed my cold and my fever. Secondly, while I was lying on the couch, sick, I had control of the television remote. That was because another adage at our house is, "If you're sick, you get the remote."

I channel-surfed like a man, running up and down the stations like a piano keyboard. I sang with *Sesame Street*. I learned how zebras live minute by minute. I was so sick I watched cooking shows. Which, of course, just made me more hungry.

I made quite a fashion statement on my hourly treks to the pantry and the medicine cabinet. When I am sick I need to be in my old raggedy beige sheep shirt. I have flowery pajama bottoms underneath with moose socks on my feet. Then I have to have a towel wrapped around my neck covering layers of ointment. (I don't know if it helps, but my mom did it when I was little.) My hair is a vision of matted curls sponging here and there.

It seems in our house we only get flu and colds every two years—just past the expiration date of the last miracle-medicine bottle. I came out of my week of sickness with an-other bit of information. Those infomercial people could sell stuff to a fence post. They could sell broccoli to a kid . . . speaking of which, I think there is some of that pasta casse-role left. You see, I am just not quite well even yet. I better feed it, whatever it is.

Read
1 Timothy 5

My prayer of joy for today:

Day 47

Second Grandchild

Tyler Lee Olmstead, our second grandson, was born on April 18. His birth was a long-awaited event for his brother, Justin. With his introduction to his new brother, Justin made a disturbing discovery: the new kid couldn't play yet. The first sibling fight was over the fact that Tyler couldn't leave the hospital and go to McDonald's for lunch.

I feel differently about Tyler's birth than I did Justin's. We have the same overwhelming sense of joy. But as we stood in the hospital corridor beside Todd looking at this hour-old little one, my soul was trembling. First with a thankful heart that he and Lisa survived his birth. There had been complications. But there was also a recognition that this baby was coming into a more unpleasant world.

"Oh, that's what all the old people say every time a baby is born," one friend said.

But I didn't say that four years ago when Justin was born. There is a fierceness in the world today. It is evident on the news, through television, newspapers and magazines.

"There is only one thing that can change the course of our nation. It is the parents of today. How they raise their children will determine the direction we take twenty or thirty years from now," said our friend, a school administrator. There are statistics that show the result of neglect. The neglect is not necessarily the lack of money or food, but the lack of love and nurturing care. Our future technology and lifestyles in this world, if our Lord tarries, will depend on what kind of persons are "manning the post."

Tyler will be one of those people. Who he is then will largely be determined by Todd and Lisa. That is an awesome task. They and many parents like them, who trust God, recognize the wisdom He alone can give. Parenting can be a path of joy when God is leading our steps. Welcome to our world, Tyler. God be with you.

Read
Psalm 127

My prayer of joy for today:

Uncle Carl

Carl Duke, one of my favorite uncles, died a few days ago. He was eighty years old. The next day, I read the *Billings Gazette* obituaries as I always do.

I can't remember when I first started reading all the deaths. And I can't tell you why I read them word for word. Most often I don't know the person. I guess I am just curious to see what others have done with the years they had. (Some daily obituary readers joke, "Oh, I just check each day to see if my name is there before I start my day!")

Uncle Carl's obituary was barely two inches long. It was the shortest on the page. Oh, it told that he was born near Nashville, Tennessee and had married my dad's sister, Lillian, on October 28, 1935. It said he had ranched and driven truck and belonged to the golf club. It gave the time of the memorial services and listed his wife and sister as survivors as well as nieces and nephews. That was it.

For eighty years—two inches. But I smiled. I knew that no obituary page could have told it all. He wasn't a joiner, so there were few clubs to list. He was self-employed, so there wasn't a list of company positions. He had no children, so we nieces and nephews were his kids.

But what a guy! He had a nickname for every member of our family. I never did find out how I got the handle "Nuisance," but that was his name for me as long as I can remember. My dad was "Wimpy," so of course my mom was "Mrs. Wimpy." I won't embarrass my family by listing them all.

Uncle Carl always smiled as I talked to him. He was interested in my life. "Well, Nuisance, what's going on down at Colstrip?" he'd ask. He always had some comment about his power bill and an energy question for Robert. With a twinkle in his eye.

He was a grand putterer. Under a car, in the garage, at the ranch or in the kitchen. And he liked dumps. He could find something usable every time he went. And his jobs! He was always off to a new scheme. The last one was a silver mine. I wish he could have really struck it rich before he left. He sure would have enjoyed telling about the "big one." He blessed my life. I know my family all feel the same. We will miss him terribly.

And he was rich. He trusted the Lord as his personal Savior. My Bible says, "And whosoever liveth and believeth in me shall never die" (John 11:26, KJV). So I know Uncle Carl is walking on streets of gold now, probably checking to see if heaven has a dump!

I don't think I will read all the obituaries anymore. They don't know that the facts "ain't half the story!"

I wonder what Uncle Carl has nicknamed Saint Peter?

Read
Proverbs 1

My prayer of joy for today:

Day 49

Standing in Grace

*"Therefore being justified by faith, we have peace with God
through our Lord Jesus Christ: by whom also we
have access by faith into this grace wherein we stand, and
rejoice in hope of the glory of God." (Romans 5:1-2, KJV)*

You can walk in joy when you understand and accept for yourself this foundational truth. We who have accepted the gift of salvation from God are justified by faith. By believing that God does what God says He will do. "That if you confess with your mouth, 'Jesus is Lord,' and believe in your heart that God raised him from the dead, you will be saved. For it is with your heart that you believe and are justified, and it is with your mouth that you confess and are saved" (Romans 10:9-10).

Justified equals made right with. Therefore we have peace with our Holy God through Jesus who died on the cross, the once-and-for-all-time, only perfect sacrifice for sin. It doesn't end there. Jesus defeated sin and death by His resurrection. He lives! We have the ability to believe, to have hope and to walk in faith through our living Savior, Jesus Christ.

And it gets even better—not only can we walk forgiven, with hope and faith—we can *stand* in grace! That is the foundation of my joy. It is not what I can do or not do. It is not where I have had victories or where I have failures. We *stand* in grace by faith in our Lord Jesus Christ. Grace. *Standing here, knee-deep in grace, allows me to rejoice in the glory of God and believe in the hope I have in His redemption and in His return. That gives me joy!*

Read
Romans 3:24; 5:15; 11:6; Ephesians 2:8-9

My prayer of joy for today:

Don't Put All Your Eggs in One Basket

I don't have an athletic bone in my body. My husband and three sons totally ignored that fact one birthday. We were living in Billings, Montana when they gave me a bicycle for a present. I am a good sport; I did not refuse their gift, although a picture of that lacy pink dress in the Hennessy department store window did float through my mind.

I practiced and practiced riding that bright yellow bike. I finally got to the place where I could ride down our street without the neighborhood kids laughing at me. I thought I was getting quite accomplished at this bike-riding stuff.

It was during one of my baking sprees (those are few and far between at our house) that I realized I was out of eggs. *I know what I will do,* I said to myself. *I will just bike over to the 7-11 and get the eggs!* I put on a new fashionable pink jogging suit with a racing stripe down the leg. Now I would even look athletic for the three-block ride to the store.

I told everyone in the store I had biked over to purchase my eggs. I think they already knew because it took me five minutes to get my bike leaned up against the store like I had seen the kids do. Also, I was panting and gulping for air.

I paid for the eggs and put them in the daisy-covered basket attached to the handlebars of my bike. I breathed a prayer and headed home.

The three-block ride went well. I was feeling quite confident. I had never done curbs before, but the curb by our driveway was just a small one. I braced myself and pointed my bike straight at it. When I hit the curb, the eggs flew up out of the basket. The blue carton of one dozen AA eggs lit on the driveway in front of my bike and I drove right down the carton, breaking every single egg.

Then I had to get the car out of the garage so I could go to a different grocery store and buy more eggs. I also had to change clothes because I didn't feel very athletic anymore.

I don't have an athletic bone in my body. I am glad God loves me anyway.

Read
Proverbs 26

My prayer of joy for today:

Day 51

Drive Carefully

JOY HINGE PIN

"He that goeth forth and weepeth, bearing precious seed, shall doubtless come again with rejoicing, bringing his sheaves with him." (Psalm 126:6, KJV)

It is a Bohleen family ritual. It started on my first solo trip up the drive to our ranch. I kept up the tradition when my name changed to Olmstead. I would say it to Robert. We said it when our boys begin to drive. Even though I have gray hair and my body is sinking into my shoes, my dad and mom still say it. It is the last phrase every time: "Drive carefully."

Is it just a Montana thing? Surely you say, "Drive carefully" to your loved ones too? We think the last thing we say is the most important. Legends hang on the last words said as a person dies. Ought we not then pay attention to the last words of Jesus here on earth? The Gospels record the words:

> And Jesus came and spake unto them, saying, All power is given unto me in heaven and in earth. Go ye therefore, and teach all nations, baptizing them in the name of the Father, and of the Son, and of the Holy Ghost: Teaching them to observe all things whatsoever I have commanded you: and,

105

lo, I am with you alway, even unto the end of the world. Amen. (Matthew 28:18-20, KJV)

And he said unto them, Go ye into all the world, and preach the gospel to every creature. He that believeth and is baptized shall be saved; but he that believeth not shall be damned. (Mark 16:15-16, KJV)

And that repentance and remission of sins should be preached in his name among all nations, beginning at Jerusalem. And ye are witnesses of these things. (Mark 24:47-48, KJV)

Peter was grieved because he said unto him the third time, Lovest thou me? And he said unto him, Lord, thou knowest all things; thou knowest that I love thee. Jesus saith unto him, Feed my sheep. (John 21:17, KJV)

So you see what was most important to Jesus was the lost. He left this world telling us to take the good news of the gospel to the world. "But sanctify the Lord God in your hearts: and be ready always to give an answer to every man that asketh you a reason of the hope that is in you with meekness and fear" (1 Peter 3:15, KJV).

That is a hinge pin of our joy: *doing what He told us to do.* Always be ready to give the reason for the hope that is in you!

Read
1 Peter 5

My prayer of joy for today:

Vessel of Clay

I found some interesting verses this week in Jeremiah 18. It says:

> This is the word that came to Jeremiah from the LORD: "Go down to the potter's house, and there I will give you my message." So I went down to the potter's house, and I saw him working at the wheel. But the pot he was shaping from the clay was marred in his hands; so the potter formed it into another pot, shaping it as seemed best to him.
>
> Then the word of the LORD came to me: "O house of Israel, can I not do with you as this potter does?" (18:1-6)

I am so glad that God does not give up on us. I am thankful that His mercy is for everyone. The Bible is full of verses that tell of God's love for mankind and how Jesus died on the cross for our sins.

We had relatives visit from California this summer. They took our picture with a disposable camera: the ones in which the film and camera are combined. We have disposable diapers and disposable razors. Disposable dishes and disposable medical supplies. The slogan for today is "use it and throw it away."

In the study of the Old Testament and the history of the chosen people, we see they would trust God and then they would turn their back on Him. They would get in trouble and then yell for help . . . from God, of course. And He would answer their call. Many times they suffered the consequences of their deeds, but God never gave up on them. He said, "I have loved thee with an everlasting love: therefore with lovingkindness have I drawn thee. *Again* I will build thee" (31:3-4, KJV, emphasis mine). He could have easily said, "I am done with you. I have had enough. You are never going to get it right!" But He didn't. And He didn't give up on David. He didn't give up on Peter. And He doesn't with us either. He says, "I will never leave you nor forsake you" (Joshua 1:5).

I have some friends who are going through some rough times. And I am sure they are not the only ones who are being plagued with illness and financial woes and family difficulties. But I know God knows. And He does not dispose of us when we falter or feel wounded or our faith runs thin.

That verse says He takes the marred clay in His hands and makes it into a better vessel. I am sure that clay pot yells "Ouch!" a few times as it spins around the potter's wheel . . . and so do I. But what peace there is in believing that the Potter knows best! He says in Isaiah 26:3 that He will "keep him in perfect peace, whose mind is stayed on thee" (KJV). That is where I want my mind to be . . . even when I am spinning, as wet clay, on the wheel.

Read
Jeremiah 18

My prayer of joy for today:

Day 53

A Revelation

While at a prayer meeting at church last week, I had a revelation. (Church is probably a good place to get one.) We were discussing becoming stagnant in our walk with God. "Why does this happen?" the pastor asked. "Why settle for less than the best?"

My revelation (which is a fancy word for a bright inspirational thought) was—the answer is my computer! When I got my computer, I followed the learner's tutorial. I mastered the basic steps quickly. After becoming efficient with the basics, I wanted more, so I took some classes. At my job, different computer skills were necessary, so I had to learn more—and it wasn't easy. I took more classes and asked millions of questions of my coworkers.

When I bought my computer I got lots of instruction books. Every time I got new software or a new program I got more books with simple (?) instructions and examples for practice. The method that most computer experts recommend is methodically going through the books and the tutorials following the steps and going over it again and again. The more you practice, the more you get out of your computer. Computers have such astounding capabilities; there is hardly a limit to what they can do. I am only limited by my lack of knowledge to explore options in many programs.

Back to the "revelation." It would be easier to stop learning and stay where I am in Computerville. I can do my writing, my bookkeeping, our Christmas letter and my tasks at work with the skill I have now. As a matter of fact, though I know less than a lot of people do about computers, I do know more than many folks. I am as proficient as I need to be.

Get the correlation to my revelation? It doesn't only apply to our walk with God. It can apply to our job, exercise program, school, marriage, parenting relationships and studies—being satisfied with where we are and not moving toward expanding our faith. Scripture says, "So then faith cometh by hearing, and hearing by the word of God" (Romans 10:17, KJV). That is moving forward.

Not moving? Stopped in my tracks? No thanks. I think I would rather be a rushing brook than a stagnant pond. Thank You, Lord, for the revelation!

**Read
Romans 12**

My prayer of joy for today:

The Frozen Turkeys

It didn't hit me until I had gone to bed and was going over plans for the next day. Our church ladies were taking a meal to a family because the mother had been sick. We decided on a turkey dinner, and I had volunteered to bake the turkey.

"YIKES!" I said as I sat straight up in bed. Robert came instantly alive. "You know what? Turkeys are frozen!" He didn't catch on. "Turkeys are frozen!" I repeated. *Lord, could You please send a thawed turkey to the Colstrip IGA?* I begged.

The next morning I was at the grocery store as the owner unlocked the doors. "Jerry, do you have any thawed turkeys?"

"Only at Thanksgiving. Not in March," he said.

"Well, then give me two turkeys quick." I figured God knew about the dinner. He evidently thought I could handle the crisis. After all, I am smart enough to know you can't bake a turkey at your house and not do one for your family. I raced home.

The microwave was out. There was no way I could smoosh the frozen turkey into it. (I tried.) I filled the bathtub with cold water. I wanted to use hot, but I didn't want to poison the people either. I alternated them between baths and showers. Rolling the turkeys around in the water, I realized one frozen turkey might be keeping the other frozen turkey from thawing out. I put ours in the refrigerator. Tomorrow I'd cook him for us.

Zero hour was 2 o'clock. I still had to get the giblet things out for the dressing. I tried everything. The icy giblets would not come out. I was desperate enough to go to the garage. I found one of Robert's car tools that had a hooky thing on it. I poured boiling water on it. (Not to sanitize it . . . I hadn't thought of that. I figured it might slide in better hot.) I got the turkey on a towel between my legs. I grabbed on to the bird with my left hand. With the tool in my right hand I pried and pulled and pushed and yanked. Out the giblets flew! I boiled them on high.

At 2 o'clock the bathing turkey was mostly thawed. I prayed over him again. After all, this was a religious mission. Then I did what you do to turkeys and put him in the oven.

At 6, I called the family and explained I'd be a little late. At 7, I took the bird out of the oven. I had a fit of giggles when I took the lid off the pan. The little red thermometer thing was out. The turkey was a golden brown and done. But in my haste to get him in the oven, I had forgotten to tie his legs and wings down. There he lay, in golden splendor with hands and feet spread wide. He looked as desperate as I felt. I tied him up so the family wouldn't be frightened when they saw him.

I must confess that I didn't sleep much that night either. I was praying for the turkey and the family. I called the first thing in the morning. They were still alive. The turkey wasn't. God had answered my prayers. When we had our turkey dinner the next night, I didn't eat much. I was kinda sick of turkey.

Read
Hebrews 4

My prayer of joy for today:

Day 55

You Better Leave Me Alone

I paid the fee and joined a ten-week diet program. I just wanted to lose ten more pounds before summer. I went to the first meeting and came home primed for victory. I set my personal food diary on the kitchen counter so I could record every morsel that entered my mouth. I got my food scale out. I was ready.

The first morning I carefully recorded ½ cup of skim milk, 3/4 ounces of oat flakes and the apple I ate for breakfast. I went out for lunch and ate a chef salad, no dressing. At suppertime I popped a dieter's TV dinner in the oven. The first day was a success.

The second day I weighed out my oat flakes and carefully measured the skim milk. At 10:14 a.m. a sack of donuts appeared at work. *I'm not having any donuts; I'm on a diet. Well . . . one donut. I'll count the optional calories. I'll skip lunch and have another donut. Now I am a failure. This day is shot. Might as well have lunch anyway. I'll write it down after supper. No, I won't eat supper.*

It's 6 p.m. I might as well fix a big supper . . . for my husband. When I decided to have the potatoes and gravy, I decided that I would get back on program the next day. I didn't want to write in my food diary. But I did.

Next morning: ½ cup skim milk, 3/4 ounces of oat flakes, one apple. I was back on track. *I can do this.* At work that morning a friend I haven't seen in a long time stopped in. "You look great!" she said. "You've really lost a lot of weight!" At lunch I was still glowing from the compliment. So I had a microwave pizza . . . after all, I looked great! Now I really had to talk to myself: *Lois, you paid good money for this program so you could lose weight. Is food all you can think about? Think about those white slacks you can't get into. Think about summer clothes. A swimsuit.* I was back on track.

Next morning: ½ cup of skim milk, oat flakes, one apple. Salad for lunch. *I can do it.* I met a friend for coffee. The waitress stood there, so we wondered, "Do we want to eat something?"

My friend said, "How about nachos supreme?"

"Absolutely," I said.

After all, I've already shot this week. I will start over next week. But could I just ask a favor of you? Don't tell me I look great if you see me, OK? It makes me eat.

But don't tell me I look a little heavier either. That makes me depressed and that makes me eat.

Maybe you could just ignore me. No, don't do that, because I might think you are mad at me and when I worry . . .

"Oh, God, I need Your help here!"

Read
Ephesians 5:1-10

My prayer of joy for today:

Day 56

Thy Word Is a Lamp

JOY HINGE PIN

"Thou wilt show me the path of life: in thy presence is fulness of joy; at thy right hand there are pleasures for evermore." (Psalm 16:11, KJV)

I was listening to Christian radio as I drove to town. "If I feed my faith, my fears will starve to death," said Pastor Stan Simmons of Faith Chapel in Billings. I shouted, "Amen! Amen! Amen!"

I have lived with that axiom since that day many years ago. I know that the root of most of our worries in life is fear. And I know that worry and joy do not rest well together. We can't have both. Therefore if I want joy, I need to eliminate worry.

You can make your own list of fear-based-worries. Mine included fear of failure, fear of unforgiveness and fear of the unknown (not knowing if I am going to get my own way?!). I put the axiom to work. I laid my fears beside the Word of God. I know that faith comes "by hearing, and hearing by the word of God" (Romans 10:17, KJV). I watched my worries creep away and faith flood my soul. Again and again I remember my position. I am a child of God (10:9-10). I have placed my feet on His

115

path with my eyes focused on Him. I feed on His Word. My fears starve to death. There is fullness of joy.

> Holding forth the word of life; that I may rejoice in the day of Christ, that I have not run in vain, neither laboured in vain. (Philippians 2:16, KJV)

> As newborn babes, desire the sincere milk of the word, that ye may grow thereby. (1 Peter 2:2, KJV)

> Blessed is the man that walketh not in the counsel of the ungodly, nor standeth in the way of sinners, nor sitteth in the seat of the scornful. But his delight is in the law of the LORD; and in his law doth he meditate day and night. And he shall be like a tree planted by the rivers of water, that bringeth forth his fruit in his season; his leaf also shall not wither; and whatsoever he doeth shall prosper. (Psalm 1:1-3, KJV)

> Thy word is a lamp unto my feet, and a light unto my path. (119:105, KJV)

> Uphold me according unto thy word, that I may live: and let me not be ashamed of my hope. (119:116, KJV)

Therein, dear friends, lies a hinge pin of our joy. *Feed on God's Word.* Dwell there. As you feed your faith, your faith will grow, your joy will grow and your fears in life will starve to death.

Read
Psalm 27

My prayer of joy for today:

Day 57

The Straw That Breaks . . .

It is amazing to me that the disagreements in a marriage are not about the big things. If we buy a house or make a career move, those we carry to God in prayer and discuss and compromise. It's the little things that threaten the marriage vows. In our home we've had an ongoing "discussion" about plastic mugs.

You know those big insulated ones you get at the gas station? We have a few hundred of them in our house. Of course I am exaggerating, but this is OK when the issue becomes a "discussion," right? It's a marriage principle.

One cupboard in our kitchen is filled with these mugs. Amazing when there are only two people living here. Every time I try to get rid of one, I hear, "Not that one. I got it at the Texaco station in New Mexico." "Not that one. That was the one Kevin gave me from his trip to Arizona." And we go down the list.

When we went on our trip to Seattle, Robert had his new (groan) green mug. It says "BP" on it. I have my coffee in my old orange and brown Town Pump mug with "Lois" written on it in magic marker. I have had it for years. (It is a matter of principle.) I knew that as soon as we got to the National Drag Races, he'd have to buy another one. I was wrong.

At the second gas stop on our trip out, he came to the car with a red and yellow mug. "Look at this," he says. "Neat, huh?"

I won't tell you what I said. Which brings me to the second principle in marriage wars. Never make an issue out of small stuff—it will come back to haunt you. We got to Seattle. With Kevin and Kelli, we were up early and on our way to the races. We stopped at a drive-in where Kevin and his dad picked a high-cholesterol breakfast.

"We'll get ours further down the road," Kelli told me. "I want to show you Seattle's neatest bagel shop."

"That should be healthy," I commented.

The shop was exquisite. The decor was country in shades of plum and green. More bagels than I had seen in my lifetime begged our attention and there were more varieties of cream cheese than I dreamed existed. I finally made my selection. Then I saw their insulated mugs . . . jade green and plum with flowers winding around the handle. The bagel shop name was on the side. "Oh, I have to have one of these," I told Kelli.

"Get it," she said.

"You don't understand," I said. "I can't."

"Don't you have enough money? I'll get it for you," she said.

"Nope. I *am* going to get it. Will you carry it out to the car for me?" She looked at me like I lost my marbles but did carry it to the car. Which brings me to marriage principle number three. You might just as well confess when you are wrong. It saves a lot of grief.

"I bought me a new coffee mug," I said.

"Oh," he said. And that is marriage principle number four. When you win, you don't have to make a big deal about it. It all evens out in the long run.

Read
Hebrews 13

My prayer of joy for today:

Day 58

A Heavenly Place

What do you know about heaven? Think about it. Give yourself some mental pictures. You could make a list using your concordance in your Bible.

Thoughts of heaven are a source of joy to me. No matter what life brings down here on earth, someday I will be in heaven. There are lots of mental pictures of heaven in my mind. I can almost feel the warmth of perfect love, the sunshine of our Savior's glory and the marvelous happiness being in God's presence. Not to mention the peace that will come as we experience sin and death being defeated forever.

Today, let's just rejoice in some heavenly word pictures to increase our joy and hope in our future:

> And I heard a voice from heaven saying unto me, Write, Blessed are the dead which die in the Lord from henceforth: Yea, saith the Spirit, *that they may rest from their labours;* and their works do follow them. (Revelation 14:13, KJV, emphasis added)

> There remaineth therefore *a rest to the people of God.* For he that is entered into his rest, he also hath ceased from his own works, as God did from his. Let us labour therefore to enter into that rest, lest any man fall after the same

example of unbelief. (Hebrews 4:9-11, KJV, emphasis added)

Take heed that ye despise not one of these little ones; for I say unto you, That in heaven their angels do always *behold the face of my Father* which is in heaven. For the Son of man is come to save that which was lost. (Matthew 18:10-11, KJV, emphasis added)

And he showed me a pure river of water of life, clear as crystal, proceeding out of the throne of God and of the Lamb. In the midst of the street of it, and on either side of the river, was there the tree of life, which bare twelve manner of fruits, and yielded her fruit every month: and the leaves of the tree were for the healing of the nations. And there shall be no more curse: *but the throne of God and of the Lamb shall be in it*; and his servants shall serve him. (Revelation 22:1-3, KJV, emphasis added)

Read
Matthew 6:20; Luke 12:40; John 14:2

My prayer of joy for today:

Linda's Coat

My friend Linda does not shop at the Used Clothing Drop Barn in the center of Colstrip even though you may have seen her there a few weeks ago. Her car was parked by the little red barn with the driver's side door open. Most of Linda's body was in the window of the barn with just her feet sticking out.

You see, the little red barn in the center of our town is for dropping off good used clothing and household goods that can be recycled. A van comes from Miles City once a week to collect the articles, and they are recycled through a used resources store there.

Linda was soon to move from our community to Minnesota to be near her new granddaughter and the rest of her family. Winters are tough there just as they are in Montana, so she saved the money and bought a new, dressier coat. Being kind-hearted and not needing her heavy work coat any longer, she decided to put it in the Clothing Barn so someone else could use it. After she washed it to give it away, she laid it on a chair to take the next day. But just like the rest of us, Linda is a creature of habit. She got up the next morning, put on the coat and went to work. "I'll drop it off on the way home tonight," she said. "Then I won't forget it again." So she did.

Into the drop window went the coat with a prayer for the person who would wear it next.

The next morning she arrived at work with no keys to get into the plant. It didn't take her long to figure that puzzle out. The keys were in the pocket of the coat which had spent the night in the little red barn. She was praying again as she sped to see if the coat was still there. She was praying for three things: 1) that the truck from Miles City had not been down to pick up stuff; 2) that the keys were still in the coat when she found it; 3) that no one would call the police and say someone was stealing from the little red barn.

The Lord answered her prayers with "yes." The truck had not been there and the coat was. The keys were retrieved with an athletic dive through the window of the barn. She got back into her car and went to work.

A week later we bid our dear friend good-bye as she moved away. God bless you, Linda. If you ever need any shopping done for you, call me. I go past the little red barn every day.

And for you reading this—laugh with us and then check your home. Are there some things that someone in need could make good use of? Visit your "red barn" and drop some gifts off today. Offer joy to someone else. Just be sure and check the pockets first.

Read
Matthew 10

My prayer of joy for today:

Day 60

God, the Author?

Y*ou should not have prayed that!* I said to myself right after I uttered the prayer out loud. The pastor had asked us to offer prayers of thanksgiving to God in church. "Lord, I thank You for watching over us and being the author of our day," I had prayed. I suppose some would think that was not a comforting prayer.

Our week had been full to overflowing. One of our well pumps burned out. A pipe sprang a leak in our root cellar, causing the second flood in two weeks. We had house guests which we had to farm out to others because we had no water. God was the author of this? Another family in our church had their daughter stranded with a broken-down car. She had to be across the state for college exams the next morning. God was the author of that? Others were facing a family death and difficult marriage and job situations. God was the author of those?

Yet my prayer was sincere. I believe that what comes into the day of a believer is only what God allows. Some days are not pleasant. Some days are hard. But God has allowed those events, for our good, for His good.

"I hate spinach. I won't eat it!"
"You have to eat it. It's good for you."

"I want to go to the party. Everybody is going!"
"No. There is no adult supervision."

"I don't want to wear a coat!"
"You have to wear a coat. It is snowing today."

Sometimes things just don't seem fair. Life doesn't always go the way we want. The Bible says, "He causes his sun to rise on the evil and the good, and sends rain on the righteous and the unrighteous" (Matthew 5:45).

The hailstorm that devastated our town a few years ago did not skip the houses of the nice, sweet people in town and break the windows of the wicked. (Besides, we don't have any wicked people in our town.)

The Bible also tells us, "Your enemy the devil prowls around like a roaring lion looking for someone to devour" (1 Peter 5:8).

God is the author of my days because He says He is. If I can trust that God has a plan for me, then when the well pump or the bank account or the relationship goes dry, or when disease or sorrows come, I face the crisis with confidence that it will all work out someday for my benefit. I may not ever know why . . . but I can trust the Author. That gives me joy.

Read
Job 1

My prayer of joy for today:

Day 61

Ice Fishing

It was the same last winter. I have never seen such a persevering bunch! Snow and freezing temperatures do not deter them. The ice fishermen are on the lake behind our house hoping for that big catch. From time to time we walk out on the lake to see how they are doing. Usually there will be one or two pike lying beside their ice hut.

"And I threw three back," they'll say. "They weren't big enough." Now, a fish that is a foot long is a big fish to me. But they are looking for something bigger. Or they might say, "Fishing hasn't been good this week." Yet that very fisherman will be back the next day, cold or not, for eight hours more.

I can't believe it! Just maybe I could get a little excited about going fishing—in the summer along a beautiful little creek with water bubbling along over the rocks and a blanket to sit on. And coffee and a picnic lunch. 'Course I'd want a good book along just in case the fishing wasn't good.

And just maybe I could even try ice fishing. On a nice clear winter day with a little sunshine (not too much sun because I still tiptoe whenever I go out on the lake, even if they tell me the ice is a foot thick). I would bundle up and take a lawn chair to sit on. And if I did just happen to catch a fish I certainly wouldn't think of throwing it back. And I would never sit out there for hours checking three strings down in the water that weren't jiggling while I was freezing to death.

Perseverance isn't just for fishermen. My husband worked all week on a carburetor. He took it completely apart and rebuilt it. The task took hours. He put it back on the truck and it didn't work.

"What are you going to do?" I asked. I was ready to offer to go buy a new one.

"I'm going to take it apart and try again." He didn't even seem discouraged. I was impressed. He was even still smiling.

I thought about how many projects I give up on. I have a dress hanging in my sewing room that just needs the hem. I didn't like the way it looked so I quit making it. I quit. I even give up on some people. I give up praying for a certain request.

Then I heard this week that somebody caught a thirty-one-inch-long northern pike last weekend in the lake. I bet there'll be 100 fishermen out on the lake this Saturday.

Maybe I better go take another look at that dress! And spend some time in prayer today.

Read
Luke 18:1-8

My prayer of joy for today:

Day 62

Lord, Help My Brain

For a really busy person, I sure have been standing around a lot lately. Standing and staring. Like yesterday. I got up, crawled out of bed, trudged into the bathroom and turned the light on. Then I stood and stared at the mirror. I knew I was supposed to do something. I just couldn't remember what it was. Finally my brain kicked into gear: "Wash your face, Lois, for a start."

It happens quite frequently. I am in the kitchen and I need to get a clean towel out of the linen closet down the hall. The next thing I know is that I am doing it again—standing and staring. "Now what did I come here for?" Most often if I head back from whence I came, I get a comic strip "lightbulb moment." Then the challenge is to race back and get what I remembered I was after—before I forget again! This brain short-circuit also happens when I am speaking to someone. I have my next thought on the tip of my tongue. Just before it is time for my next thought to be eloquently spoken, it skips off my tongue. The words just float a few inches away from my face. I know they are out there. I can feel them. I just can't get them to return to my brain so they can fall out my mouth.

I'm starting to sound like my parents. Or, worse yet, my whole gang of relatives at a holiday dinner. It starts simply: "I ran into old . . . oh, you know . . . that guy we bought the green pickup from. . . ."

"I know who you mean . . . he was married to the sister of that old guy who ran the feed store . . ." responds Uncle Sonny.

Aunt Helen says, "No, she wasn't his sister—she was the daughter of his brother who moved into the old Harley place. . . ."

"No," my dad will chime in. "That brother was the one who took Lillian up to Willow Creek, remember? He didn't have a daughter. That was that blonde schoolteacher's sister. . . ."

By then I have lost track of who they were originally trying to name. I just stand and stare. Hey! That's where I get it from—it's my heritage! I get it from my uncle . . . you know the one, he lives up the creek from those people that bought the old Nelson place. . . .

Dear Lord, oh please help my brain. You promised to give wisdom liberally to those who ask. I need wisdom and I need it liberally ('cause I'd just like to have a little to give my aunts and my uncles and my . . .). Well, just send some. I can't remember who I was going to give it to. Amen.

Read
James 1:5; 3:17; Proverbs 4:7; 9:1

My prayer of joy for today:

Day 63

Salvation—Rejoice!

ƆOY ƕINGE PIN

*"Yet I will rejoice in the LORD, I will joy
in the God of my salvation." (Habakkuk 3:18, KJV)*

A birth is a miraculous event. I stand in awe of the magnificence of a tiny "seed" becoming a bouncing, beautiful baby. But there is another kind of birth, one about which Nicodemus asked,

> How can a man be born when he is old? can he enter the second time into his mother's womb, and be born? Jesus answered, Verily, verily, I say unto thee, Except a man be born of water and of the Spirit, he cannot enter into the kingdom of God. That which is born of the flesh is flesh; and that which is born of the Spirit is spirit. Marvel not that I said unto thee, Ye must be born again. (John 3:4-7, KJV)

God gave His only begotten Son as the once-and-for-all-time sacrifice for our sin. He calls it a gift. "The gift of God is eternal life through Jesus Christ our Lord" (Romans 6:23, KJV). This is the ultimate love gift. Even more amazing is the fact that God joys in our salvation—in our accepting His gift!

"The LORD thy God in the midst of thee is mighty; he will save, he will rejoice over thee with joy; he will rest in his love, he will joy over thee with singing" (Zephaniah 3:17, KJV).

Now think about this. You heard the Word. You asked Jesus into your life. There was a new birth. God got a hold of your life. You accepted His gift. You surrendered control. "Behold, God is my salvation; I will trust, and not be afraid: for the LORD JEHOVAH is my strength and my song; he also is become my salvation. Therefore with joy shall ye draw water out of the wells of salvation" (Isaiah 12:2-3, KJV).

You want to grow and be all God wants you to be? *Rejoice! Rejoice!* Have joy in your salvation. *Rejoice!*

> For the exciting of our thankfulness, and the quickening of our diligence, it is good for us to consider what means we enjoy, and what discoveries are made to us, now under the gospel, above what they had, and enjoyed, who lived under the Old Testament dispensation, especially in the revelation of the atonement for sin.*

Rejoice! Therein lies the source of my joy! *I am following the psalmist: "Then will I go unto the altar of God, unto God my exceeding joy: yea, upon the harp will I praise thee, O God my God" (Psalm 43:4, KJV). Rejoice! Rejoice!*

Read
Isaiah 12

My prayer of joy for today:

Matthew Henry's Commentary on the Whole Bible, New Modern Edition Electronic Database (Henrickson Publishers, Inc., 1991). Used by permission. All rights reserved.

A-h-h, Married Life!

If you are married, you will appreciate this.

Harold is an avid hunter, so each year when hunting season approacheth, the scouting of the back roads in the area becomes an obsession. Sue goes with him as they scope the countryside for game.

On this particular day, they were up in a canyon. It was a steep road, one of those that hugs the mountainside and drops straight off the other side down to the creek. The road was ice-covered from an early fall snowstorm.

"I better get out and turn the hubs in," said Harold. "This is steeper than I thought."

He put the truck in neutral and set the emergency brake before he got out. He got down on one knee by the front wheel. Then, horror of all horrors—the truck started to slide! The sunshine on the ice-covered road and the steep incline combined to make a crystal ice ramp out of the road.

"At first, I just froze," Sue told me. "Then I attempted to get out of my seat belt, over the video camera, my purse, our lunch and all the stuff on the seat between me and the steering wheel and the brake. Harold had grabbed on to the door of the pickup but he was just sliding along with it. I knew I didn't dare look down. It was a long, long way to the bottom!"

Somehow, the pickup turned just a bit and backed into the mountain side of the hill. There they stopped. Both Harold and Sue said they hadn't breathed the entire time. It was quite a scare. The fear of what could have happened filled their minds. Well . . . until Harold made it back into the truck, let out a huge sigh and said, "I could've lost my truck!"

Ain't marriage grand?!

Read
1 Samuel 25

My prayer of joy for today:

Grandpa's Flight

The whole family was encouraging our eighty-one-year-old Grandpa to take a trip to California to see his brothers and sisters. We finally convinced him that flying would be the quickest and most comfortable way to go. He decided to give it a try, halfway. He would go down by car with some friends, stay two weeks and fly home before it was time for plowing.

At 8 a.m., after a joy-filled reunion and a week of visiting, he boarded the plane in Los Angeles for the trip home. Actually it was his second trip to the airport. He had missed his flight the day before but his luggage hadn't.

It was a three-hour flight to Montana. My mom left the ranch at about the same time to drive to the nearest airport, an hour away in Belgrade, to meet his plane. Meanwhile, Grandpa was putting the napkin on his lap for breakfast. However, instead of five sourdough pancakes, ham and eggs, it was juice and a small sweet roll. But the view was supposed to be good. He looked for Salt Lake City and didn't see it. It was under fog. So his plane flew to Denver. At the Belgrade airport, Mom learned the flight was delayed so she went back home. Grandpa was still flying over Colorado and Wyoming with a few more down and ups and delays.

Somewhere he was served a light lunch, for it was now noon and he was still flying the skies. The seat was getting a little smaller and more cramped. My dad and Uncle Sonny made the next trip to the Belgrade airport in the late afternoon. But Grandpa had changed his plans. He heard the pilot say they would be landing in Billings and he decided then and there to get off that plane before it got rerouted somewhere else. "I have a granddaughter who lives there," he told the concerned stewardess. "That is where I am getting off."

"This is the ——— Airlines," the caller said when I answered my phone. "I am calling on behalf of Mr. Bohleen. He says you are his granddaughter and he would like you to pick him up right now." After a hasty call to the ranch to let my parents know our lost traveler had his feet on the ground, I headed for the airport. Grandpa was standing at the gate, leaning on his cane. His beard was two days old. He was ready for a decent meal. The next day, I took him to the train station. He rode the last 100 miles of his trip closer to the ground.

On the way to the train station we had passed a huge billboard advertising an airline. In huge, bright red letters, it said, "The Only Way to Get There Fast!" My dear saintly grandpa didn't say a word, bless his heart. He had long ago learned that some days just go different than we plan.

Read
Acts 9:1-31

My prayer of joy for today:

A Cup of Cold Water Is Hot Soup

I read somewhere about a father who came into the living room where his son was sprawled on the couch watching television.

The father said, "In twenty-four hours you won't even remember what you are seeing now. How about doing something for the next twenty minutes that you will remember the next twenty years? I promise that you will enjoy it every time you think of it."

"What is it?" the son asked.

"Well, there's several inches of snow on old Mrs. Brown's walks," the father said, "Why don't you see if you can shovel it off and get back home without her knowing?"

The son did the walk in fifteen minutes.

"Mrs. Brown never knew who did the job," the son related years later. "Dad was right. It's been a lot more than twenty years and I have enjoyed the memory every time I've thought about it."

I can attest to the same experience with different circumstances. I was on the receiving end. It was 1964. Colstrip was a hub of activity during the construction of the steam-generating plants. Most of us had just moved here. Adjustments were being made by people who had left their homes and families in other places. Friendships were just being formed. There were no stores, doctors or shopping malls. Enough telephone lines were not available yet, so we had no phone. Television reception was sporadic. And I got the flu!

There were three little boys at home who depended on me and I felt rotten. I missed my friends and family. Robert was immersed in his work and spent long hours there. I tried to get up off the couch and get to the door when I heard the doorbell ring, but I couldn't make it in time. When I got there the person had already left.

Sitting just outside the door was a pot of soup. Hot, home-made soup. I looked up and down the street but there was not a person in sight. I never found out who left the soup.

And I have never forgotten that act of kindness. They must have read the Bible verses in Matthew 25:35-40 and Matthew 10:42 that tell us to offer a cup of cold water in Jesus' name. Do you suppose He also meant hot soup?

Read
Matthew 10:42; 25:35-40

My prayer of joy for today

This Is the Day

♂OY ₭INGE PIN

"This is the day which the LORD hath made;
we will rejoice and be glad in it." (Psalm 118:24, KJV)

I often hear myself saying, "Thank You, Lord, for allowing me to live that I might experience this day." Do you ever say that, or is it just us cancer people? Do people have to go through a near-death crisis in order to have a thankful heart for a new day? I hope not. The Bible says, "This is the day which the LORD hath made; we will rejoice and be glad in it" (Psalm 118:24, KJV). This is a step of obedience, a way of life, that we can choose to follow.

I loved hearing Joyce Meyer say, "In my early years as a Christian, I used to wake up, thinking about the day ahead and dreading it . . . just like I did before I became a Christian. It took me many years to wake up praising God. Now I think about the day, thank God for it and praise Him for being alive to serve Him!"* Amen and Amen!

That is a sign of Christian maturity. Paul addresses immaturity with the Corinthian church: "I gave you milk, not solid food, for you were not yet ready for it. Indeed, you are still not ready. You are still worldly" (1 Corinthians 3:2-3).

Christian maturity is being sanctified (made holy) by faith in Jesus Christ. *We walk in joy and thankfulness for every day we are given to serve God.*

That is a hinge pin for joy. That is foundational to our walk with joy. And foundational to a victorious Christian walk. Today we are going to read our Scripture out loud with a thankful and joyful heart, OK?

Read
Isaiah 12 (KJV):

And in that day [I shall] say, O LORD, I will praise thee: though thou wast angry with me, thine anger is turned away, and thou comfortedst me. Behold, God is my salvation; I will trust, and not be afraid: for the LORD JEHOVAH is my strength and my song; he also is become my salvation. Therefore with joy shall ye draw water out of the wells of salvation. And in that day shall ye say, Praise the LORD, call upon his name, declare his doings among the people, make mention that his name is exalted. Sing unto the LORD; for he hath done excellent things: this is known in all the earth. Cry out and shout, thou inhabitant of Zion: for great is the Holy One of Israel in the midst of thee.

My prayer of joy for today:

* Joyce Meyer, *Life in the Word* (television program).

Day 68

Country School Valentines

Attending a two-room country school was part of my heritage. There were eighteen kids in the school when I started first grade. We hadn't crossed too many days off the February calendar before I realized this Valentine business was a big deal. The big kids (those in grades 6-8) talked about little else at recess—who was going to send a card to whom. And, "Ha, ha, ha, I'll bet you get a card from . . ."

It got worse as the day drew near. The teacher didn't help either. She directed the decorating of a big box. We covered it with red paper and cut out hearts and pasted them on the box. It was a technical project as we had to leave an opening for the cards to be dropped through. The big kids figured that out. Then it was placed on a desk at the front of the room. Staring at us. The teacher said everyone had to make a card for each student in our school. Our moms were given cookie and Kool-Aid assignments. There would be a party with games.

I worried. I had a crush on a boy in third grade. He was the bravest (he caught frogs out of the slough by the school) and the nicest (he helped me feel better when I was always the last one picked for a baseball team during recess) boy at my school.

I practically wore out the punch-out cards and glue-together envelopes as I went through them at home, night after night, trying to find the perfect one. (My little brother, Ronnie, who wasn't in school yet, thought this was a new card game like Old Maid.) I finally made a decision on the card for my special friend.

The day of the party I wore a dress to school. We played Fox and Geese at recess. I couldn't concentrate. The party started right after lunch. We pushed all the desks back. I opened each card very carefully. My card to my friend was one of the first to be delivered. He looked at me, held it up and said, "Thanks, Lois." I got one from him too. It had Mickey Mouse on the front. Alas, the love connection didn't last out the week. But I remember thinking this Valentine's Day wasn't so bad after all. I felt so good that I even took a sprinkle-topped cookie home in my lunch pail for my brother.

You know, joy comes with kindness. They are partners. Maybe there is someone around me—or you—today who needs a sprinkle-topped cookie, someone who isn't going to get a Valentine from anyone else.

I'd best stop typing. I think I will bake some cookies.

Read
Ruth 3

My prayer of joy for today:

140

Day 69

Keeping Up with the Seniors

Each year I make goals for my health: to keep up a good exercise program, eat healthy and maintain the right weight. This is not easy for a confirmed non-athletic, rather compulsive person.

I thought I would try a new exercise regimen. A friend gave me a Racquel Welch exercise video tape. I figured we were close in age so this might be OK. I was going to start the next day but the video started with Monday so I had to wait for Monday. I forgot about it until the following Thursday, so then it was the next week before I started. I faced the television screen at 6:30 on Monday morning in my sweats. The session was supposed to last fifteen minutes. I lasted nine. I am not mature enough to watch someone seven years older than I am look that good *and* be able to lay her palms on the floor while standing up. I gave the video back to my friend. I decided to continue walking for exercise.

Another part of my goal had to do with losing ten pounds. April 1 was my D-Day. Then I remembered we had our tax appointment that weekend. I knew I should not add dieting to tax stress. So I started on April 4.

A week later I was happy with my resolve. I was actually making progress. I think I will be able to live to a healthy old age, Lord willing. I may even get energetic enough to keep up with the active senior citizens group in Colstrip. I was watching them bowl one day while I ate my lunch—lots of lettuce with none of the stuff I really like on it.

They must really practice good health habits to be that energetic, I thought. I ate my salad with gusto—until those seniors took the booth next to ours and had lunch. They had cheeseburgers and fries.

Read
Daniel 1

My prayer of joy for today:

142

Day 70

Rescued

The need of a Savior became apparent to me when I was twenty-six years old. Oh, I knew about Jesus before then. I was a church person. I was very nice most of the time. It was just that I had never surrendered control of my life to God. I was still trying to please Him with my good works.

A perfect illustration comes to me in those 911 television programs. We watch breathlessly as a victim floats down a flood-swollen canal clinging to a twisting log. A helicopter hovers overhead, trying to match the speed of the person floating helplessly in the muddy water. We sit on the edge of our chairs as the drama is played out on the screen. We see a cable being let down from the helicopter to the desperate person. We can't help yelling, "Grab it!"

This is the moment of extreme terror (or ultimate faith) when the person has to let go of the log and grab the cable. Yet the only way salvation will come to the victim is when he lets go of the temporary safety of the twisting log and grabs onto the rescue cable. "Ahhh," we say, "he made it!" One of the key elements in the rescue is the realization of the person in the water that he needs to be rescued—or saved. That way he will be ready to let go of the log and put his life in the hands of the safety crew in the helicopter.

This is an incredible picture of the gospel of the Bible. God, our Creator, knew we could not save ourselves. Mankind couldn't even keep the ten rules brought down the mountain by Moses. Each one of us, especially me, can testify to how futile are our attempts at goodness to measure up to God's standard. So the message brought to the shepherds by the angels, "Today in the town of David a Savior has been born to you; he is Christ the Lord" (Luke 2:11) is a "rescue helicopter" for us. A way to live. A way out of the "floods of despair and helplessness" common in the world today. Our part is letting go of the log of trying it our own way.

What or whom are you trying to hang on to for salvation? Are you barely clinging to a log? It was over thirty years ago when I knelt beside my bed and prayed, "Lord, I see now I need a Savior. I need saving—mostly from myself and my futile attempts at holiness. Please forgive my sin. Come into my life and take control. Amen." That was the day true joy walked into my life.

Read
Romans 6:23; 10:9-10; Ephesians 2:8-9

My prayer of joy for today:

Day 71

The Parking Lot

The husband and wife arrive in the family vehicle at the mall parking lot. The parking lot has space for 1,200 cars, give or take a few. This morning there are several empty spaces. He-who-is-driving turns into the wide middle aisle. There are two empty spots on this end. She-who-must-not-tell-him-how-to-drive says nothing as he drives by the empty spots. She just sets her lips in a straight line.

Another spot is open halfway down the lane. She-who slants her shoulder slightly to the left to prepare for his turn into the spot and then stiffly straightens up as He-who drives on. There is one on the right two car-lengths down. Just as He-who puts on the brakes to pull into the spot, a little red coupe cuts the corner and dives into the spot.

"Those little cars ought to be outlawed," says He-who.

"I think there is one right over there," says She-who, breaking her oath not to say one word about driving or parking on this day.

"I don't like to park over there. Those trees drip sap on the pickup."

There must be a secret homing device for each man for his particular vehicle, thinks the woman to herself. *The male bird cannot rest until he is at his own nest which has a secret beeper heard only by the male of the species.* "Hmmmmm."

145

"Hmmmmm what? I couldn't park there! Didn't you see that dented and beat-up truck parked right there? No telling how that person would back out of that spot!"

"Hon, I didn't hmmmm you. I was just hmmmm-ing to myself."

"Oh well, here's one. Finally. Now, what did you have to do here?"

"I just have to drop these glasses off. It will only take a minute."

"Well, why didn't you say so? I would have just parked in the front and waited for you."

"Not a chance," She-who says. "I wouldn't miss touring a parking lot with you!"

Read
Proverbs 2

My prayer of joy for today:

Day 72

Mom, the Patient

I went home to the ranch not to visit, but to be a nurse for my mom, who had surgery. I know she would have rather been branding or even middle-of-the-night, freezing-weather calving than being the Patient. Lying on the couch is something she has never done so I was worried about how we'd do. But she was a trooper and did it with grace and faith.

Going to town and buying personalized blue badges on which I had engraved, "Lois—Nurse" and "Lorraine—Patient" was my first step in planning ahead. I had to keep telling everyone in the hospital how old she really is for fear they would think she was the daughter and I was the mom. I wavered in my assigned job as Dad's nanny. You remember cooking is not my specialty. I think he was scared too. He stopped at the store on the way home and bought five cans of Dinty Moore stew.

He will have to give me credit, though. The second batch of scrambled eggs was excellent. And I was honest enough to tell him the first batch was in the garbage. As it was, I know Mom was lying on the couch praying for herself as Dad and I stumbled through the kitchen, banging pots and pans, trying to figure out what to cook and how to run the oven. It was a blessed week and we appreciated the time together.

It is hard to be the Patient, especially if you are the Mom. The home doesn't seem to function normally when Mom is out of commission. The biggest hassle for a mom is letting go of responsibility and resting. Someone sent me the following note in an e-mail message. Moms—and dads . . . well, all of us ought to pay attention:

> Do not feel
> totally
> personally
> irrevocably
> responsible
> for everything.
> That's My job.
> Love, God

When you find yourself in a position of illness or recuperation from a tragic event, bear in mind that God does allow us to go through times of rest. Remember Psalm 23:2: "He leadeth me beside the still waters" (KJV)? If we, the patients, accept our time of rest in patience (like my Mom, the Patient, did), it will be a gift of joy for those who are the care-givers (like me, the Nurse).

Read
Mark 5

My prayer of joy for today:

Day 73

Enjoying the Trip

We moved nine miles north of Colstrip on July 2, 1995. We love our place in the country. On one of my first trips out to our new place with a load of our stuff, I made a special request to God. I prayed, *Dear Lord, please let me always enjoy and appreciate this nine-mile trip. Don't let me be rushing into town or rushing home and not see the sights. Amen.*

You see, I know myself. I can get so wrapped up in the goal at hand that I do not see anything but the road. This was not a prayer to be an unsafe driver. It was a prayer to be a vigilant one. Montana is called the "Big Sky Country." In eastern Montana it is truly that. In the nine miles we travel there are hills covered with pine and spruce trees and juniper bushes. There are several ranches with cows and horses in the pastures. Armells Creek meanders through the valley by the highway so we see herds of deer and antelope often. Now and then we get a glimpse of coyotes (the duck-eating variety), but I am not quite as thrilled with them. As the seasons change, so does the landscape. It is a wonderful drive.

I confess sometimes I forget and just hustle to town or back home. But most of the time, I do appreciate the drive because I remember that I prayed for this awareness. Today I had a lunch date. We are having a late fall with cold nights but no snow. There is ice on our pond except where the ducks are swimming in shifts to keep a small spot open. So I wasn't surprised to see ice on the pond by the McDonald ranch. Then I saw the horses. I signaled, slowed down and pulled over to the side of the road.

Because horses are not as diligent as ducks, this pond was frozen over. There were five horses trying to break through the ice to get a drink. They had been using their hooves to no avail. As I watched, four of the horses gave up and loped over to the gate. I surmised they decided to wait for man-help. The tall roan with two white stocking feet kept trying. By the time the other horses were at the gate, she had broken the ice. She drank until she got her fill, then leisurely joined the rest of the horses standing at the gate. I had to get to my lunch date, so I pulled back on the highway. Which was fine. I got the point of the horse-sermon right away. I drove on with a joyful heart. *Thank You, Lord. Once again I am glad You kept my eyes open. Four horses are still thirsty. The one who persevered beyond the rest got her thirst quenched. Amen!*

Read
Judges 7

My prayer of joy for today:

Day 74

The Ole Gunny Sack

Does this sound familiar? You are sitting at the table with your beloved spouse. It is a run-of-the-mill day. He says something like, "Did you remember to get coffee today?" and before you know it, it is like someone set off a keg of dynamite.

One little comment lights the fuse, such as "Did *you* forget to take the garbage out?" or "Don't I have *any* clean underwear?" or "Are we having meatloaf *again?*" A dead-sure explosive fuse can be "There is *how* much left in the checking account?"

Some people believe the touchiness of a situation is all in the timing—there are good times and bad times to bring up certain subjects. That may be true. But when it comes to marital disagreements, I subscribe to a different philosophy. I believe in the gunny sack theory myself.

I first heard the gunny sack theory from a marriage counselor from Denver, who gave a marriage seminar in our church years ago. "Each of us is given an invisible gunny sack," Rev. Crabtree said. "When you stand at the altar repeating those vows, you are issued your own personal gunny sack." He said it hangs over our backs and most of the time we are oblivious to its presence even though we may use it several times a day.

We walk through the day with our beloved. She says, "Are you going to mow the lawn?" He thinks, *She doesn't think I have enough to do! Now she's nagging me about the lawn!* He answers her with, "I'm going to get at it tonight." Her remark gets tossed into his invisible gunny sack. Along with the comment about the socks on the floor she mentioned earlier. Those remarks nestle down in the sack with the burnt toast for breakfast and getting in the car and finding the gas tank empty again.

Her sack has a few bundles in it too. He mentioned his mother's cooking. He still hasn't fixed the toaster. Two days ago he said, "We have to spend less money," and today he brought home three new fishing flies he had to have. Into the sack!

So these two are each carrying around a gunny sack of unresolved hurts, and it is full and ready to burst. That explains why married folk can have a major disagreement over something like just a cup left on the coffee table. The gunny sack just wouldn't hold one more thing. And usually once we start unloading our gunny sack we can't stop until the whole sack is empty. One partner is amazed at what is being dumped . . . then decides to unload his gunny sack as well.

When the gunny sacks are empty, forgiveness and reconciliation can come. Married bliss can return as the issues are dealt with, compromises are made, wounds are healed and apologies wash over the hurts. Maybe the secret to happy relationships is being aware of the gunny sacks we carry and just tearing a small hole in the bottom. I believe God told us to treat each other with love and forgiveness.

Marriage counselors hold seminars. Psychologists write papers on marital difficulties. Maybe I should let them know it's just those gunny sacks!

Read
1 Corinthians 13

My prayer of joy for today:

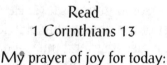

Day 75

My Birthday

My odometer turning over another number didn't upset me this year. I wasn't upset because I had made a discovery earlier in the month. I have discovered I really like the age I am now. My friends had royally roasted me on my half-century birthday a few years ago with fifty black balloons, crazy gifts and a horrid picture in the area newspapers. Yet that year turned out to be a blessed one, as have these since.

I have said that the thirties were my favorite years. (Not the 1930s, but *my* thirties.) But they are being rivaled by my fifties. There are some really great things about this stage of life. I thought about that when I left the motel for a speaking engagement one night. I slipped into my raincoat. I have an actual raincoat of my own now! And I snapped a button on my umbrella and walked across the street in the pouring rain. Not only do I have an umbrella now, but I know where it is and that it will work. It hasn't been used to build a tent for toy soldiers or a net to catch butterflies or worse yet, frogs.

I have change now. If someone comes to the door wanting a donation or selling cookies, I can actually find a dollar or five to give them. I can remember school day mornings frantically searching through pockets, the junk drawer and the jar by the washing machine for two quarters for lunch money. There were about twenty years where I don't think I ever had a dollar in my pocket. And if I did, someone under four feet tall was asking for it.

You know what else? When I go to the cupboard, the groceries I bought yesterday are still there. My radio dial stays on KURL, the Christian radio station I listen to. It hasn't even heard rock music . . . and the earphones still work. When the phone rings, the calls are for us. The interior of the car stays clean. Flies don't get in the house because someone left the door open. The towels are hanging neatly on the rods for that purpose in the bathroom. I can find my hair spray and my blow dryer. I don't have to hide the chocolate chips. I can walk through the living room without jumping over highways made of dominos and bridges of toothpicks. There aren't little cars and trucks parked in front of Lego houses. . . .

Would you please excuse me? I have to stop right here. There are tears running down my face.

I think I'll call the boys—just to see how they're doing. . . .

**Read
Ecclesiastes 11**

My prayer of joy for today:

Honestly

I have a very unusual phobia. I am scared of fish. I am scared out of my ever-loving mind of fish. I am terrified of fish. Yes, I am a Christian woman. If God calls me into this kind of fishing, He will provide a miracle. I believe it.

I don't dream about sharks or whales. It is not the big fish that scare me. It is the little and medium-size fish. Do not judge me too harshly. I am not afraid of spiders, mice or snakes. I am not afraid of water or flying. I do not freeze up when speaking before crowds or when I peer over the edge of the Space Needle.

I just have totally white-face, white-knuckle, screaming-out-of-control fear of fish. But it is not all fish. I like to eat fish—fried trout is a favorite. I can even fish. I am *not* afraid of worms, so I can bait my own hook. I can sit on the bank and patiently wait for a fish to bite. But once the fish is hooked and comes out of the water, I need assistance. Someone else has to take the pole because I am gone. As in not there anymore.

My family is well aware of my peculiarity. They can tease me about my cooking or my driving or anything else—we just don't joke about fish. Once we tried lake fishing. My husband should have known better than to put three boys (ages six to twelve), four fishing poles, lunch, two oars and a crazy woman in a boat!

To make a long story short, two fishing poles went to the bottom of the lake and Kevin got caught by his ear with a flying hook. Robert said he didn't know whether to call the Fish & Game Commission, 911 or a psychiatrist!

Our grandson Justin got a fishing game for his birthday last week. It came with batteries, twenty smiling plastic fish and four poles. "Play with me, Grammi?" he says.

This may be the cure. I can't let Justin think his Grammi is an idiot!

Read
2 Timothy 1

My prayer of joy for today:

Day 77

Fixing Wrongs

Standing on your soapbox can irritate some people. I found that out recently. First I have to tell you that I don't drag my soapbox out often. God has given me a very diplomatic spirit. Seeing both sides of an issue comes quite easy most of the time. But recently I got out my soapbox for a weekly column in our local newspaper. It was three short snippets about some current issues in our community. I thought it was quite lighthearted and cute. A few hours after the paper came out, my editor called.

"You got the senior citizen group riled up," she said. "They didn't like your column."

"I'll call one of them right away," I said. It didn't take long to discover that my comments about the change in their eating place did not sit well. My column had said how much we would all miss them since they would be eating at the senior center now. They wanted me to realize that most of them really liked their new digs. They loved the food and being together. They invited me to lunch the next day. I went and it was very nice. They didn't feed me crow, either! I apologized and put in a quick call to the editor to put a public apology in the paper.

Having opinions and sticking with them is a healthy attribute. However, I am a Christian first, a columnist second.

Christians are not allowed to have broken relationships if we can help it. "Therefore if thou bring thy gift to the altar, and there rememberest that thy brother hath ought against thee; leave there thy gift before the altar, and go thy way; first be reconciled to thy brother, and then come and offer thy gift" (Matthew 5:23-24, KJV). Our good intentions do not matter. Being defensive is not an option.

A few weeks later, I met one of the senior citizens in the grocery store. She was still upset. I apologized again. Jesus taught us in the Lord's Prayer how to pray about broken relationships. There are many verses that clearly state we are to be about the business of loving and serving—and forgiving, just as He has forgiven us. When we hurt someone, we are to seek forgiveness.

I have had lots of practice in this area because I can easily open my mouth and un-thought words just fall out! Evidently my keyboard caught the disease from my mouth! The neat part of this experience is that I know God loves me. He is teaching me. The soapbox lesson was well-learned. I plan on going to the senior citizens' again for lunch. I have friends there. They know I make mistakes, yet they still like me. Being forgiven gives me a joyful feeling.

Read
Matthew 5

My prayer of joy for today:

Day 78

My Mom's Mouse Mission

My mom might need some of the extra old work clothes I have. It seems my mom was on a Mouse Mission. We folks in the country know how those critters look for warm people-type homes in the winter. Diligent, as always, she was going to eliminate any access routes for the critters this fall. She checked the entire crawl space under their log home. There would be no hantavirus-carrying rodents in her house.

She was using a spray can of foam insulation. A drill bit could not forge a doorway through that yellow-lather stuff after it hardens. She used up the first can on possible entry sites. When she tried to put the second can into gear, it would not spray. She crawled up from under the house and went into the garage. Tools of various kinds were tried to no avail. (My mom is one of those women to whom God gave the gift of mechanical wizardry.) The nozzle was plugged tight with the guck.

If you have lived on a ranch, you know that baling wire fixes everything. So she got a piece of baling wire and shoved it down the spray spout. Sure enough, the baling wire did the trick. Real well! Yellow foam was erupting like Old Faithful from the can. She ran out into the yard trailing mustard goo. When the eruption got done, Mom had the look of a loser in a fight at a hot dog stand.

Besides being diligent, my mom is thrifty. She wasn't going to lose a good pair of Levis. That took priority over her war on mice. She hung the pants on the fence. Knocking the rock-hard yellow goo off with a stick didn't work. She went to Plan B. (Did I mention she can "figger" a solution to any problem?)

Solution: She got a blow torch. Heat would melt the yellow warts on her pants.

Safety Precaution: She laid the garden hose by the fence. Just in case.

Mistake: The blow torch solution.

With a careful aim she fired at the yellow globs. Which instantly turned to black globs. *Just a little more heat,* she thought. Up two notches on the blow torch. Aim. Fire.

Yup—fire. Smoke came rolling out the top of the pants! Hose. Water. No more smoke. I don't know when she thinks she will wear the cut-offs. No one has ever seen my mom in short pants.

Read
John 10:10; 6:12b; Job 22:20

My prayer of joy for today:

Day 79

Any Idols?

King Jehoshaphat became a role model and inspiration to me during my cancer treatment. I learned so much from his experiences. Using these lessons brought many blessings to me. One of the things I love about God's Word is that the people whose lives are chronicled are not larger than life. God doesn't just tell us all the good stuff.

Blunders, mistakes, rebellion and battles lost are included with the stories of victory and miracles. God clearly shows us that He can use the "weakest vessels." Like Moses who said, "Who am I, that I should go to Pharaoh?" (Exodus 3:11). Like Mary who said to the angel who came to her, "How will this be?" (Luke 1:34) and like Jonah who said (basically), "Nah, Lord, I don't want to go to Nineveh."

When God wanted to use King Jehoshaphat for a special task, He knew the king was not perfect. He even told him so. But God also said, "Nevertheless there are good things found in thee . . ." (2 Chronicles 19:3. KJV). God used Jehoshaphat to bring victory to the nation of Judah in spite of the odds. It was three against one. The Ammonites, the Moabites and the army of Mt. Seir were all coming for battle. God used the faith of Jehoshaphat and his people to bring about a great victory, and they didn't even have to lift up a single weapon except their voices. You can read about that yourself in Second

Chronicles 19 and 20. You would expect after this awesome victory that Jehoshaphat would lead a perfect life, never turning from his Lord. Did you read what happened? He let idols stay in his country and he formed a friendship with someone of bad influence.

We would never do anything like that! We would never give our lives to the Lord, receive blessings and victory, then fall prey to the devices of wicked influence . . . would we? The very notion of idols fosters thoughts of pagan cannibals. Certainly there are no idols in our culture. In our lives. We just wouldn't allow evil to sway our convictions . . . would we?

It is disappointing to me that Jehoshaphat failed to yield totally to His God. But the *greatest sadness would be if,* as I read and study his life, *I allow the same mistakes in mine.* That would be a major obstacle in my path of joy.

Read
1 Corinthians 10

My prayer of joy for today:

Mudder Mothers

I was on the first level of scaffold with my perfa-taping tools and a pail of "mud." I had been assigned this seaming job because I have no fear of heights, having gotten my wings on the old barn at home. Only on the barn I was not perfa-taping with a tray of mud in one hand and the tape and trowel in my other hand. It had occurred to me quite quickly that a woman my age could break her neck from ten feet up. I pushed fear aside with a prayer. I finished my circle around the dome in a few hours. I did the perfa-taping without any bubbles this time. As a matter of fact, quite professionally, I thought.

Randy, the church building foreman, gave me a thumbs-up sign. The men brought another three-foot section of scaffold for the next level. Up I went with my stuff and another prayer.

I was a little surprised at the butterflies in my midsection. *I am not afraid of heights,* I reminded myself. It took me a little longer to make my taping loop around the dome. I think it was because I was holding on more.

The next day I got another section of scaffold. An eight-foot section. (In case you weren't paying attention, ten plus three plus eight equals twenty-one.) It takes ingenuity to get a human body from the top rung of the ladder onto the flat metal surface of the scaffold twenty-one feet up when neither your hands or feet want to let go. *Move your stiffened fingers inch by inch,* I tell me. *Slide your belly onto the top, bringing the heavier part of your body along. And pray your feet are coming too.*

We (me, the tools, the mud and the roll of perfa-tape) made it! But I cannot make my body do what my brain commands. When I breathe, the scaffold shakes. My butterflies want *down.* "Everything OK up there?" someone yells.

"Oh yeah, sure, fine, fine." Fear of losing one's reputation is a tremendous motivator. I started to work. I prayed. I sang religious songs. I prayed some more. I did all the sheetrock seams in the tiptop of the dome. Pastor Norm came up to see how I was doing. The only thing scarier than being on the top was two people on top. But I was a gracious hostess and my perfa-taping passed inspection.

Donna was on another scaffold three feet below. We wrote new words to "Shall We Gather at the River?": "As we climb upon the scaffold; with our mudders and our pails; praying fiercely as we're climbing; Lord, why didn't You give us tails?"

Now the lesson: The first level was a little scary. But when they put the next section on, that first level was a breeze. When the third section went up, the second section became safe. Do you suppose fear of new "heights" is keeping us from some great adventures? Like pressing on in that job? Swimming? Losing weight? Making that new acquaintance? Writing that letter? Trusting God in your impossible situation? Haul out another section of scaffold . . . and keep climbing!

Read
Micah 4

My prayer of joy for today:

All Men Shall Know

JOY HINGE PIN

"A new commandment I give unto you, That ye love one another; as I have loved you, that ye also love one another. By this shall all men know that ye are my disciples if ye have love one to another." (John 13:34-35, KJV)

"I buy this, even though it is very expensive, because my mother wore it," Julie said.

We were at the perfume counter in a pricey department store. I would have bought it also after she said, "My mother died when I was in high school. I always loved the perfume she wore. Smelling it reminds me of her. It was years before I found it. And still years later," she laughed, "before we could afford it."

Sweet aromas are pleasing to our senses. They waft through the air and linger.

Then Mary took about a pint of pure nard, an expensive perfume; she poured it on Jesus' feet and wiped his feet with her hair. And the house was filled with the fragrance of the perfume. . . .

"Leave her alone," Jesus replied. "[It was intended] that she should save this perfume for the day of my burial. You will always have the poor among you, but you will not always have me." (John 12:3, 7-8)

Therein lies another hinge pin of my joy. Jesus said He would not always be here to walk among men. But we are. We are here walking around this earth. And there is an aroma. The "scent or flavor of that aroma" is a choice He leaves to us. There is no middle ground in our Christian testimony. We can have a pleasing aroma to those around us or we can have an offensive, negative one.

Now get the wondrous truth of this concept: I can, simply by acting in love and kindness, let people know that I, Lois, am one of Jesus' disciples! Isn't that miraculous? I don't have to wear a badge, a uniform or a monogrammed T-shirt—people will know I am one of His by my love.

Now, wouldn't you just suppose *joy* enters into that reputation as well? It does. *Knowing that I can be a witness for my Lord and Savior by loving others fills me with joy.* The joy spills out of my love for Jesus. That is foundational to Christian maturity.

Read
John 21:16; 1 Corinthians 13:1; 1 John 3:14; 4:20

My prayer of joy for today:

Sin Junk

Junk is a sinister enemy. It creeps up on you. It is self-propagating. In the country, you have a gully dump. This is where you place the stuff you want to get rid of when you don't have time to haul it away right then. Only you don't get rid of it. It grows.

Out here on Golden Pond, we designated 1999 as the year to get rid of the junk. We were amazed how it had taken over our place. We hauled trailerload after trailerload to the dump. Over 6,000 pounds of it was loaded piece by piece on the trailer and hauled to the dump where we unloaded it and drove away in relief. Only to discover there was more. There must be something magical about old defunct engines, transmissions and axles. First you have one, then you have two. Two turns into four, four into eight . . . well, you get the picture. We hauled the junk eighty miles to Pacific Steel in Miles City. They must want it, because they paid us a fee for giving it to them. But they did not pay much—the payment did not quite equal the price of the gas and lunch for the trip. But He-who was very happy. "It feels so good to be rid of it!" he kept saying on the way home.

I couldn't help but apply a spiritual lesson. If someone had told us to move over three tons of junk off our place this summer, we would have trembled in our boots. But because we did a little over several weeks, it was a manageable task.

Do you suppose that is why God teaches us and leads us in our lives step by step, day by day? If we saw ourselves as He sees us, our sin would be insurmountable. So He, in grace and mercy, works with us, by His Holy Spirit, just a few "pounds" at a time. He brings a wrong attitude to light. We deal with it, asking Him to forgive us, and He cleanses that sin from our lives. Then a problem with envy jumps up. We didn't recognize it. Was it hiding in a gully? So we confess that. He cleanses us and restores our righteousness before Him.

Junk overtakes our lives, weighing us down, dirtying our landscapes. We need to have a cleanup day, a purging, just like hauling away the old car parts. Then we can echo Robert's words, "It feels so good to get rid of it!"

Maybe our lesson for this week should be checking our property—do we have some junk that needs hauling away? See you at the dump! I'll be there! God says in First John 1:9, "If we confess our sins, he is faithful and just to forgive us our sins, and to cleanse us from all unrighteousness" (KJV).

God just reminded me that impatience belongs there. I'm taking that to the dump and we ain't hauling it back home.

Just as with a junk pile, you have to start somewhere, or the junk will stay forever. Why not make today the day? Start by talking to God—prayer. It will feel so good to get rid of the junk!

Read
1 John 1

My prayer of joy for today:

Shall We Gather at the River

Phyllis gave me permission to tell this story. It has to do with a sinkful of dirty dishes. She had been so busy there had been no time for dishes. (I had to say that. She is my friend.)

She took all the dishes out of the sink. She put the plug in the sink and added a generous squirt of soap. She turned the water on. Immediately, that flow of water reminded her that she needed to move the sprinkler hose in the garden. She ran out the back door. She was walking back to the house after moving the hose when she took a good look at her flower bed beside the house. "These really need weeding! I should just do it right now!" She got down on her knees and went to work.

She was almost done with the job. "All I have to do is put some water on these and I will be done with this . . . water? WATER!"

She went running, well, sliding into the kitchen. There was water everywhere. It had run behind the toaster, around the blender, trickled down the drawers and flooded the floor. It took over an hour to clean up the mess. When she got done, she had the cleanest kitchen in Colstrip. She put all the towels and rugs in the washer. Then she stood in front of the sink once again. She put the plug in the sink and added a generous squirt of soap. She turned the water on. The telephone rang. It was her sister, Linda, in Ohio. Phyllis couldn't hear her sister very clearly. The water was making too much noise. So she stepped into the bathroom off the kitchen and shut the door. . . . She did!

And this story always makes me feel better when I do something similar! Our joy does not depend on our circumstances! Thanks, Phyllis.

Read
Psalm 1

My prayer of joy for today:

Day 84

Weak Faith

The last time I was that scared was in 1959 during the Montana Hebgen Lake earthquake. I mean quaking-in-your-bones scared. I was seventeen then, living on the ranch less than 100 miles from the epicenter. The earthquake woke us up when our house rolled and shook.

This time I was in Giddings, Texas. My husband and I were on a trip. We rented a car after our plane landed in Houston to drive to Austin. I had said "no" when the rental agent asked about insurance. "We have our own that covers our driving," I said.

The rental agent countered, "For $11.95 the entire price of the car would be covered." He added, "You never know when the car might just disappear." So I agreed and we bought the insurance.

It was about 6 p.m. when we were approaching Giddings that we heard the tornado warnings on the radio. I asked Robert to pick a motel that was low and solid. The sky was black and in five minutes it turned from day to night. I had dressed up for our flight (we did that back in those days) but the minute we got into our motel room, I put on my jogging suit and tennis shoes. I didn't want to face a tornado in high heels. The TV kept broadcasting weather alerts, but the green sky was warning enough for this ranch kid from Montana. Lightning flashed continually and would blacken the television every few minutes. Frantic prayers were sent heavenward but my faith was weak—I was scared silly. Terrified.

171

The skies opened their faucets and rain poured down. I had never seen rain like that. The parking lot looked like a swimming pool within minutes. Robert was standing outside the motel door saying, "Isn't this fantastic! Look at that lightning!" I was frantic. Should the window be opened or closed? Were you supposed to hide along the north or the south wall? Then I heard an alarm go off outside. *This is it. Our time has come,* I said to myself. The night before we had all three of our boys together for supper. We had a delightful time together. *That was just like something the Lord would do,* I thought to myself, *getting us together for one last meal so the boys can have happy memories of us. And that rental agent said something about cars disappearing down here in Texas.*

I was ready to beg Robert to pull the mattress over our bodies when he walked in the door. "Did you hear that alarm? The lightning set off a car alarm."

"It wasn't the Lord calling us home to heaven?" I asked.

I felt like the storm lasted ten years. As I untied the laces on my tennis shoes and reached for my nightgown, I told the Lord I hadn't exercised much faith in the crisis. I guess He probably already knew that. *It was just so unnerving to me. I never was in an almost-tornado before,* I prayed in my defense.

Then I thought of Second Corinthians 12:9, "My strength is made perfect in weakness" (KJV), and realized that is the kind of thing God specializes in. When we are weak, He is strong.

Read
Psalm 46

My prayer of joy for today:

Day 85

Alone Together

We have entered a new era in our home. We are alone. *Alone together*. Just him and me and the two cats and twenty-six ducks.

Our sons are officially raised. (I think. At least they are no longer here for meals.) The oldest has a job and his own apartment. The youngest started college this fall. He now has his own pad. The middlest son graduated from college in June. He spent two months at home while seeking a job. That two months endangered our mother-son relationship at many times, but we did survive. Now he has a job and a pad too.

This first night of *alone together* should have been a special occasion. We had looked forward to this for twenty-six years. No, that is not true. We did not start looking forward to being alone until we had teenagers. But with each progressing year, *alone together* kept looking better. Right now let me state that we dearly love our children and almost all of the time. But the idea is to raise them up and then they leave. Then the father and mother can spend some time together with the love they share that started this whole thing to begin with!

I knew I should cook something special and have candles and a tablecloth and all . . . but I was just exhausted. The summer was not easy. I reheated some leftover hot dogs. Robert said he didn't mind. He was exhausted too. After supper he stretched out on the couch. I curled up on the loveseat.

Our first night *alone together* after all these years. He slept. I slept. Finally we got up and went to bed and slept. Have you ever heard of jet-lag?

Read
Deuteronomy 33

My prayer of joy for today:

Day 86

Funnel or Sprinkler?

A re you a funnel or a sprinkler at church? Do you say, "Feed me"? Are you constantly grading the pastor and the church to see if your needs are being met? Or do you consider your church a place where God can use you to minister to others?

Church families are a unique grouping of people. God places people with different talents within a church body so that each can have a unique part in making the whole function in unity for His glory. The needs of the church are many. There have to be preachers and teachers, evangelists and givers. There have to be those that show mercy and love. There have to be those that handle the business matters and those that do the music. There have to be those who fix up and those who clean up.

God's Word says, "For as we have many members in one body, and all members have not the same office: So we, being many, are one body in Christ, and every one members one of another" (Romans 12:4-5, KJV).

We can focus in or we can focus out. Granted, we each have times when our needs are great and we need the ministry of the body.

However, by the power of the Holy Spirit, our main purpose is serving one another. I don't know how far I would get taking a funnel out to water our lawn. Our sprinkler does a much better job. When we operate as unique vessels, showering others with the gifts God has given us, joy happens. We produce fruit. Which are you—a funnel or a sprinkler?

Read
Matthew 12

My prayer of joy for today:

From My Bottom Rung

Do you ever talk to the Lord when you drive? (I didn't ask if you talk to the Lord when someone else is driving. A lot of people do that. I have done it myself.) Do you ever talk to God when you are in the car by yourself?

I do. I have found that it is a great way to spend precious time praying and praising and singing and listening and meditating with the Lord. You have to keep your eyes open, of course!

On a recent trip to Bozeman, a five-hour trip from home, I was quietly reminded of me-with-an-attitude problem, a problem of putting myself a rung higher on the ladder than someone else. Since I figure I'm only on the first rung of the ladder, that meant I put this other person right down in the dirt.

You don't need to be trying to figure out who it was. You probably don't know him. He was one of the shaggiest, dirtiest, scariest hitchhikers I have ever seen. He was standing alongside the road by a stop sign as I prepared to reenter the highway at Columbus after getting gas. As my finger instinctively went to the door auto-lock button, my mouth went "yu-uu-ck!"

And just as fast as that sensor sent an electrical impulse to that door switch, God sent an even more powerful impulse into my mind, *And just who do you think you are, Miss Bottom*

Rung? Tears came to my eyes immediately. Sometimes I think God will never get me molded into a faithful servant! I still am learning the basics.

As I glanced back in my rearview mirror, I could see the man standing in the rain with his two big bags of possessions at his side. He didn't look scary anymore. I knew as if God had spoken to me out loud that this man was loved by God. I don't know if that man knows it or not. But I know it.

"Lord, I guess I look a whole lot better than him on the out-side (I had a new red-and-white sweater and pants set on). But right now I feel like the inside of me is pretty dirty, shaggy and scary! Please forgive me!" You know how sometimes you get that well-washed-in-Tide feeling when a truly repentant prayer comes from your lips? I felt cleansed . . . and forgiven. I drove on down the highway awfully thankful that God loves because of who He is, not because of who I am. "And by the way, Lord, it sure would be nice if You sent someone to pick that man up. And would You let him know that You love him if he doesn't know it?"

As I prayed (eyes open), I was looking up from where I sit on my bottom rung . . . and it felt good. I didn't know that there was still another lesson waiting for me—down another road.

Read
Luke 10:30-37

My prayer of joy for today:

Day 88

'Twas a Good Bad Week

It all started with a lovely idea. Phyllis and I could stay in our trailer in the Big Horn Mountains of Wyoming for a day before we were scheduled for speaking and singing at a retreat at a camp nearby. We could rest.

However, soon after we arrived, the lovely idea fell apart. There was a malfunction with our gas furnace. It happened while I was lighting the pilot light. There was a *boom* and a blowtorch flame. My glasses were blown six feet down the hall. My face, my hair and left hand were closest to the flame. Our first prayer was one of thanksgiving. It could have been worse. We treated my burns with our first-aid kit. Later in the day, Phyllis trimmed my burned hair with my sewing scissors. She did a good job too! The next day the furnace repairman came up the mountain and fixed the furnace. That evening we drove to Camp Bethel where 115 ladies met us at the retreat. The theme of the retreat was "Becoming a Woman of Grace." Enough said.

On Sunday, we finished the retreat. Our first stop at home was the clinic. Robert met us there. It was not fun getting the burns on my hand treated, but I did find out I could pick between green, purple, pink, blue or fluorescent orange bandages. I picked purple. You know that poem about old ladies and purple?

On Tuesday, I locked the keys in our pickup at the Coal Bowl. The deputy came to help. He didn't give me a ticket for stupidity. That night, we left for Billings. I was driving when a pheasant flew across the road and I ran smack into him. The impact broke the grill on our truck. It also took out some other stuff. It is a good thing we hadn't taken the car instead.

On Friday, no fooling, I locked the keys in the car at the laundromat where I was washing the bedding from the trailer. I called Robert. He brought his keys to unlock it. I was being so careful; I don't know how I did it. It has been years since I locked the keys in any vehicle. I think I need help!

Do you ever have a bad week? I think I just had mine. But I thank God that it all turned out OK and that it was not worse. I have to say it was a good bad week!

Read
James 1

My prayer of joy for today:

Where's the Cake?

Do you sometimes feel like a total failure? I do.

Late Saturday afternoon, I went to get my hair cut. As she was cutting my hair, Kris said, "I hear today is Robert's birthday."

I said, "Yes, we went out to supper last night. I found a tape he wanted. I am giving him that for his birthday."

Then she said, "What kind of birthday cake did you bake?"

I froze. I was so quiet, Kris repeated the question. I finally found my voice. It was tangled up with my heart, which was sinking into my stomach.

"Kris, I didn't. I forgot. I forgot all about a birthday cake!"

I just sat there thinking, *Lois, you dummy. The man you love with your whole heart, the father of your children, that precious man—and you did not even remember the most traditional part of birthdays—THE CAKE!*

Depression was folding her arms around me. Kris was laughing. "Well, he knows how you cook. He probably wouldn't even want a cake, right?"

I agreed with that statement, but I have always bought the birthday cakes. I could've remembered to do that.

When Depression knows she has me, she doesn't stop with the first accusation. It is always followed with former failures, "Lois, if you could cook like everyone else, you could bake a cake." And then, "You are such a poor wife. Look at all that man does for you and he has to ask six times before you remember to mend his shirt." After a few moments of contemplation, I was able to reel off what seemed like 100 failures in my mind. I was sinking fast. *Lois, you are no good. You will never amount to anything*. And that dour thought was followed by, *Who could love you, anyway?*

I walked out of the beauty shop looking great—on the outside. I raced straight to the grocery store. "Praise the Lord," I said. They had his favorite, chocolate cake with chocolate icing. I paid for the cake and headed home.

As I walked into the house, Robert met me at the door. Tears welled up in my eyes just at the sight of him.

"What have you got there?" he asked.

"Your cake, your birthday cake," I said.

"Great!" he said. "You know what? I totally forgot about a cake!"

Standing right there in the kitchen I wrapped my arms around him. I gave him a big kiss with tears running down my face. Oh, how I love that man. He was looking kind of bewildered by all this emotion over a store-bought birthday cake.

Depression was slinking out the kitchen door. She could see her victory was gone. I was still hugging the man I love. "I love you and I am so glad God led us together. He knew we would be a team. He knew you were for me," I said.

I closed the door behind my unwelcome guest with a final shove: *Yes, I am a failure in some areas. I have got so much to learn. But I am trying. God isn't finished with me yet!*

Read
Hebrews 13

My prayer of joy for today:

182

Day 90

Three and Up

JOY HINGE PIN

"Make a joyful noise unto the LORD, all ye lands. Serve the LORD with gladness: come before his presence with singing. Know ye that the LORD he is God: it is he that hath made us, and not we ourselves; we are his people, and the sheep of his pasture. Enter into his gates with thanksgiving, and into his courts with praise: be thankful unto him, and bless his name. For the LORD is good; his mercy is everlasting; and his truth endureth to all generations." (Psalm 100, KJV)

It is a rite of passage. Getting old enough to take the kids back to see the "old home place." My grandfather, my dad's dad, came to Forest Grove, Montana, with his family, livestock and possessions loaded in a train. (My great grandparents came from Sweden.) Later the family moved north of Livingston. A few years ago, four generations of us made the trip to Forest Grove to look at the old home place, the school, the cemetery and the church. We had a whole caravan of cars filled with relatives.

The church was locked. Mr. Isaac opened it up for our entourage. It is a very small, beautiful church. The old kerosene lights and the pump organ are still there. The high-back wooden pews reflected the rainbow rays coming through stained glass windows. "We still have services here," Mr. Isaac said. "Ministers rotate coming out from Lewistown every Sunday."

"How many people come to church here?" I asked.

"Three and up," he said.

It was one of those epiphany moments in my life. Three and up. Not "Oh, we never have many," or "Oh, we just have two or three." He said, "Three and up!"

Right then, I asked my Lord and Savior, "Heavenly Father, make me a 'three and up' kind of person. Make my heart always see the bright side, the right side. Make me always be a reflection of your joy." That day a change came in my life. This book is a result of that day. Psalm 100 became another hinge pin in my life. *"Serve the Lord with gladness!"*

Thanks, Mr. Isaac!

Read
Psalm 35

My prayer of joy for today:

To contact Lois about a speaking engagement,
write to her at

P.O. Box 907
Colstrip, Montana 59323

or e-mail her at

olmstead@mcn.net